How to Build a Better Vocabulary

by Elizabeth A. Ryan

Troll Associates

Library of Congress Cataloging-in-Publication Data

Ryan, Elizabeth A. (Elizabeth Anne), (date)
    How to build a better vocabulary / by Elizabeth A. Ryan.
      p.   cm.—(Student survival power)
    Summary: Presents tips on how to build your vocabulary. Includes
review quizzes.
    ISBN 0-8167-2460-1 (lib. bdg.)   ISBN 0-8167-2461-X (pbk.)
    1. Vocabulary—Study and teaching (Elementary) [1. Vocabulary.]
I. Title. II. Series.
LB1574.4.R93 1992
372.6'1—dc20   91-3136

Contents

Introduction:
Why Build a Better Vocabulary?
(What's in It for *You*?)

Your *vocabulary* is the total of all the words you know: the words you can recognize, the words you can understand, and the words you can use. The larger your vocabulary is, the better you are able to use words in reading, writing, and talking.

A better vocabulary will help you to enjoy reading more. You will be able to read more books more easily, because you will understand more of what has been written. Likewise, a better vocabulary will help you to feel more confident meeting more people—and different types of people. You'll feel easier in different types of conversations, knowing you can understand more words and thus better follow what is being said.

It's a funny thing about improving your vocabulary: the better it gets, the better you feel about it. If you are happy and confident in the size of your vocabulary, you'll find you are more confident even with the words you *don't* know. The confidence will make it easier to ask people what a word means if you don't recognize it, or to take an educated guess about a strange word you run across while reading. Having a good vocabulary doesn't mean knowing every single word in the dictionary—nobody's vocabulary is that good! What it does mean is that you feel confident about reading new books and meeting new people, because you feel confident about understanding most of the words and about getting more information on those you don't understand.

As you will see, words can be fun! The best way to build a vocabulary is to find ways to enjoy playing with words, because when it comes to using new words, that's just what you will be doing—playing. For example, the underlined words in each group of sentences below are very similar, but there is a difference between each of them. Can you tell what it is?

I am <u>slender</u>.
You are <u>thin</u>.
He is <u>skinny</u>.

I am <u>confident</u>.
You are <u>proud</u>.
She is <u>arrogant</u>.

I am <u>friendly</u>.
You are <u>eager</u>.
He is <u>pushy</u>.

In each of the groups, the sentence beginning with *I* has a positive quality, the sentence beginning with *you* has a somewhat less positive quality, and the sentence beginning with *he* or *she* has a downright negative quality. A good vocabulary makes it possible to tell—and to express—the slight differences in meaning between *eager* and *pushy* or between *confident* and *proud*.

6

How to Build a Better Vocabulary
(Six Tricks You Can Use)

People who want better vocabularies often try to memorize long lists of words. If you enjoy doing this, go ahead. But if you don't—don't worry. There are other ways to build your vocabulary than sheer memorization. In fact, the more you enjoy building your vocabulary, the better you will remember the words you learn.

Here are some ways of building your vocabulary:

1. *Use the Context.*   The *context* is the environment in which your word is found. Sometimes you can guess the meaning of a word just by the way it is used. For example, can you figure out the meaning of the underlined word in this sentence?

> The raincoat turned out to be <u>impermeable</u> to the icy sleet and strong winds, so Poindexter arrived home warm and dry.

From the *context*, it sounds as though *impermeable* is describing the word *raincoat*. The sentence tells us that the *impermeable* raincoat did not let in any sleet or wind, so Poindexter could stay warm and dry. So we might guess the meaning of the word as the quality of shutting things out.

> The raincoat turned out to be <u>able to shut out</u> the icy sleet and strong winds, so Poindexter arrived home warm and dry.

In fact, *impermeable* actually means, ''not allowing liquids to pass through'' or ''impenetrable (unable to be penetrated),'' so this guess is pretty good. In any case, making the guess allows us to continue reading with a pretty good understanding of what the author meant; and the next time the word *impermeable* appears, it won't look so unfamiliar.

In fact, using the context is not only good for guessing new words, but also good for remembering them. If you make a little mental picture of Poindexter wearing the raincoat through the sleet and cold winds and you attach the word *impermeable* to the picture, the chances are pretty good that you will remember the word much better than if you had just memorized it off a list. However, if you have memorized the word off a list, make up a context for it. Create a mental picture to go with the word, so that all you have to do is "look at" the picture to remember the definition of the word.

2. *Use a Dictionary or Thesaurus.* Of course, if you don't know a word, the most efficient way to find out what it means is to look it up in the dictionary. However, don't just read the definition. Create a context for it. Memorize a sentence, make up a word picture, or invent some other association that will help you remember the definition once you have learned it.

Another way to build your vocabulary is to look up a familiar word in a *thesaurus.* A thesaurus lists groups of words with similar meanings. The *synonyms* (words with similar meanings) on page 6 were found in a thesaurus. Chapter 1 has more information on using dictionaries and thesauruses.

3. *Understand How Words Are Put Together.* Many words are made up of more than one part, and each part has its own meaning. For example, the word *prediction* means a statement about the future.

The word is composed of the following parts:

pre = before
dict = something that is said
ion = an ending that shows that the word is a noun

So a prediction is something that is said or talked about before it happens. Knowing the word parts can help you make a guess as to the word's meaning; but, more important, it can help you remember that meaning once you have learned it. For more about how words are put together, see Chapter 2.

4. *Associate Words in Groups.* Many words are put together from the same word parts, with only slight variations. Once you have learned one word from a word group, it becomes much easier to learn the rest of the "family." For example, how many of the words in this group do you know?

receive	reception	recipient
deceive	deception	deceiver
perceive	perception	perceptive
intercept	interception	interceptor

All of these words include a word part that comes from the Latin verb *capere*, meaning "to take." You probably already knew the meaning of the word *receive*, but did you know that *recipient* means "the person who receives"?

> The *recipient* of the award will be flown to Hollywood, where he or she will *receive* the money.

By knowing that *recipient* is in the same family as *receive*, you've broadened your vocabulary with very little work! For more about word groups, see Chapter 3.

5. *Understand Synonyms and Antonyms.* *Synonyms* are words whose meanings are the same or very close. For example, the words *admire* and *respect* are synonyms. *Antonyms* are words whose meanings are opposites or at least very far apart. The words *alive* and *dead* are antonyms, as are the words *advance* and *retreat.* Knowing words with the same or opposite meanings can help you to remember a word's meaning. For example, if you learn the meaning of the word *beautify*—"to make beautiful"— you might learn a few synonyms along with it: *adorn, decorate,* and *embellish.* Each of these words has a slightly different meaning, as you will see if you look them up in your dictionary. However, despite these different shades of meaning, the words all belong together, and they are all antonyms for the words *mar* and *deface.* For more about how to use synonyms and antonyms to build your vocabulary, see Chapter 4.

6. *Use Word Histories.* Many words have interesting histories from literature, mythology, the Bible, or history itself. If you know the story attached to a word, you're almost certain to remember the word's meaning. For example, do you know what the word *gargantuan* means?

Gargantua was the name of a giant in a book by the French author Rabelais. So the word *gargantuan* means "huge" or "gigantic."

> After running the cross-country race, Juliet Little found that she had a *gargantuan* appetite.

For more about words and their histories, see Chapter 5.

How to Use This Book
(Can You *Really* Skip Chapters?)

At the end of this Introduction, on pages 12-22, are ten quizzes, each on a different aspect of building your vocabulary. Some of the quizzes are followed by suggestions and chapters you can refer to. We encourage you to take each quiz and follow the suggestions at the end. If you do well on a quiz, you might want to skip the chapter it refers to—or you might enjoy reading that chapter anyway.

You can also use the Contents to identify different aspects of building a vocabulary that are covered in this book. Turn to the chapter that seems to relate most to your interests.

Of course, you can always start reading Chapter 1 and read straight through the whole book! If you do so, however, remember that this book is about *building* a vocabulary, not about testing your current vocabulary. You aren't supposed to know all the words in this book. You're only supposed to get some helpful hints on how to learn more words, now and throughout the whole time you spend reading and writing.

As you will see from the Contents, this book also contains chapters on foreign words, words often confused, difficult pronunciation, and spelling. You can use these chapters as references even after you have finished reading through this book.

Building a vocabulary can be one of the most enjoyable parts of reading and writing. Try to have fun with this book. Because the more you enjoy learning a word, the more likely you are to remember it, to use it well, and to expand your own powers of reading, writing, and talking.

Ten Quizzes to Test Your Vocabulary

Remember: The purpose of these quizzes is not to give yourself a good or bad score. These quizzes are here to help you decide how best to use this book—and to introduce you to some new words! You might enjoy taking these quizzes again after you have read the book, and perhaps again after a few weeks or months, just to see how much your vocabulary has grown.

Turn to pages 22-24 at the back of this chapter for answers to all quizzes.

I. Difficult Words

Match the word with the letter that best expresses its definition.

1. perverse
   a. stubborn   b. left-handed   c. complicated

2. implacable
   a. smooth;   b. well-placed   c. unable to
      lacquered   give in

3. synonym
   a. words to a song   b. a word that means the
                            same as another word
         c. single; standing alone

4. archaic
   a. old-fashioned   b. arched   c. leaky

12

5. biceps
   a. arm muscles   b. buffalo   c. dinosaur

6. oligarchy
   a. a church ceremony   b. government by
                                 a small group
             c. a scientific process

7. arrogance
   a. cleanliness   b. readiness   c. pride

8. optimum
   a. the least   b. the best   c. the most

9. panacea
   a. a cure-all   b. a plumed hat   c. a big wave

10. bonanza
    a. a lucky break   b. a southwestern ranch
                c. a brand of steak

If you had trouble with any part of this quiz, you may want to look at Chapter 1: Aids to Building a Better Vocabulary.

II. Words in Context

Here are some words used in context. That is, they're used in an environment—a sentence. See if you can figure out the correct definition of the underlined word from the way the word is used.

1. The vivacious Vivian smiled brightly, tossed her head, and talked a mile a minute.
   a. depressed   b. frightened   c. lively

2. Marmaduke went into a long monologue about his adventures while the rest of us waited

13

for him to finish talking.
a. one-person speech   b. tiny room
         c. argument

3. In *Great Expectations*, Pip's <u>benefactor</u> gives him the money to become a gentleman.
a. banker   b. father   c. helper

4. Marty is an experienced guitarist, but he is a <u>neophyte</u> on the dance floor.
a. star   b. newcomer   c. expert

5. The tour guide gave us a <u>devious</u> explanation of how he had gotten lost.
a. uncomfortable b. not straight c. not level

6. The dentist carefully <u>extracted</u> the tooth from Matilda's mouth.
a. pulled out   b. cured   c. filled

7. The landlord will <u>evict</u> you if you do not pay your rent!
a. praise   b. prosecute   c. throw out

8. With <u>infinite</u> patience, Lola spent hours caring for her sick grandfather.
a. endless   b. brief   c. happy

9. After hearing about the accident, the firefighter was <u>galvanized</u> into quick action.
a. frightened   b. bored   c. shocked

10. That <u>tawdry</u> jacket is not worth even $10.00.
a. elegant   b. cheap   c. valuable

Figuring out words' meanings from their context is one of the best ways of building your vocabulary. However, sometimes you have to use a dictionary or thesaurus to find just the right definition or word. Chapter 1 will tell you more about aids to building your vocabulary; the rest of this book will give you clues about different types of words.

III. Greek and Latin Roots

Many words in English come from Greek and Latin. Do you know the meaning of these words?

1. derogatory
   a. insulting
   b. daring
   c. secondary

2. bicentennial
   a. once a year
   b. once every 100 years
   c. once every 200 years

3. microcosm
   a. a tiny world
   b. a small, glass dish
   c. a greenhouse

4. omnipotent
   a. weak
   b. one-sided
   c. all-powerful

5. hierarchy
   a. rule by men
   b. a system of rank
   c. a church ceremony

6. anticlimax
   a. cure for poison
   b. set of rules
   c. letdown

7. descend
   a. a side trip
   b. come down from
   c. go up to

8. dictum
   a. an absolute ruler
   b. words to write down
   c. order or rule

9. optimist
   a. someone who sees the best in everything
   b. someone who sees the worst in everything
   c. someone who is blind

10. antonym
    a. a word that means the opposite
    b. a word that means the same
    c. a word that sounds the same

You don't need to study Greek and Latin in order to speak English! Just go on to the next three quizzes to learn more about how understanding Greek and Latin word parts can help you build your vocabulary.

IV. Prefixes

A prefix is the part of the word that comes *before* the root, or main part of the word. Understanding what the different prefixes mean can help you figure out and remember the meaning of a word. This quiz will show you how helpful an understanding of prefixes can be.

Match the words with their definitions.

1. biweekly	a.	the place to go out
2. triweekly	b.	to go forward
3. pentagon	c.	to go off in another direction
4. octagon	d.	to go backward
5. progress	e.	to take back
6. regress	f.	to take out
7. digress	g.	twice a week
8. egress	h.	three times a week
9. extract	i.	eight-sided figure
10. retract	j.	five-sided figure

As you can see, just one little change in the prefix can change the whole meaning of the word! To find out more about prefixes, see Chapter 2.

V. Word Groups

Some words go together because of their *roots*—the original Greek or Latin word from which they came. Knowing what different roots mean can help you recognize and understand the meaning of many English words. This quiz will show you how an understanding of roots can help you build your vocabulary.

Match the words with their definitions.

1. subject	a. energy
2. suspect	b. alive; important
3. convict	c. bright
4. collaborate	d. comes at the end
5. compare	e. has an end
6. vital	f. dominate
7. vitality	g. mistrust
8. vivid	h. work with
9. finite	i. contrast to
10. final	j. prove guilty

Check your answers on page 23. For more about roots and word groups, see Chapter 3.

VI. Synonyms and Antonyms

Words that have the same or similar meanings are called *synonyms*. Words that have different or opposite meanings are called *antonyms*. Understanding synonyms and antonyms can be a fast way of expanding your vocabulary, as well as improving your understanding of each word.

A. Synonyms

Match the word with its synonym.

1. mar
   a. deface   b. destroy   c. detract

2. obstinate
   a. stupid   b. quiet   c. stubborn

3. assent
   a. climb   b. agree   c. reason

4. inadequate
   a. insufficient   b. inhibited   c. inevitable

5. deliberately
   a. carefully   b. accidentally   c. expertly

B. Antonyms

Match the word with its antonym.

6. attract
   a. interest   b. repel   c. excite

7. restore
   a. repair   b. replace   c. eliminate

8. condemn
   a. praise   b. ignore   c. dislike

9. minority
   a. organization   b. race   c. majority

10. frequent
    a. infrequent   b. often   c. usually

For more information about using synonyms and antonyms to build your vocabulary, see Chapter 4.

VII. Word Histories

One fun way to build your vocabulary is to learn something about the history, or etymology, of a word. Knowing a word's history can help you to remember its meaning.

Below are some words and their histories. Choose the correct definition.

1. <u>Crestfallen</u> refers to the way a rooster's crest droops after it has lost a fight. The word means
   a. excited   b. nervous   c. disappointed

2. The Romans discussed public business in their marketplace, or <u>forum</u>. Today a forum is
   a. a newspaper   b. Roman chariot
        c. any place to discuss public business

3. The Greek god of medicine, Asclepius, named one of his daughters Panakeia. A <u>panacea</u> is
   a. a cure-all   b. a Greek island   c. a doctor

4. Captain Charles Boycott was an Irish land agent whom local farmers refused to deal with after he raised rents. A <u>boycott</u> is
   a. a farmer   b. an organized refusal
        c. a plan to raise rents

5. Hackney horses pulled carriages and were often tired out. A <u>hackneyed</u> phrase is
   a. bright and interesting b. old and worn-out
        c. short and to the point

6. Samuel Maverick was a Texas rancher who refused to brand his calves. A maverick is

    a. an outlaw   b. a fool
                c. an independent type

7. Greek poets used to play the lyre while they recited. Lyrical poetry is

    a. musical   b. boring   c. read out loud

8. Nicholas Chauvin was a soldier in Napoleon's army who worshiped Napoleon above everyone else. A chauvinist is

    a. a proud patriot   b. an unthinking patriot
                c. a frightened patriot

9. The Spartans were a people of ancient Greece who lived very simply. Spartan conditions are

    a. poor   b. dangerous   c. luxurious

10. Luigi Galvani studied electricity. To galvanize someone is to

    a. interest   b. shock   c. depress

For more on words and their histories, see Chapter 5.

VIII. Words From Foreign Languages

Many words in English come from other languages. Some of these words have become so much a part of English that we have forgotten their origins. Others still seem "foreign." You need to know at least some of these words just to read the newspaper! Do you know these?

Match the words with their definitions.

1. junta	a. expert
2. détente	b. small group
3. apartheid	c. summary of work
4. kibbutz	d. stereotyped expression
5. résumé	e. small store
6. cliché	f. policy of segregation
7. bodega	g. collective farm
8. boutique	h. small store
9. ersatz	i. false
10. virtuoso	j. relaxation of tension

For more about these and other "foreign" words, see Chapter 6.

IX. Words Often Confused

Some pairs of words are easy to confuse, either because they sound the same or because they sound very similar. Here are some easily confused words. Can you tell them apart?

1. prosecute	a. to come into another country
2. persecute	b. to leave from another country
3. aisle	c. height or greatness
4. isle	d. work of art
5. complement	e. to oppress; to harass
6. compliment	f. to take to court
7. emigrate	g. passageway
8. immigrate	h. island
9. stature	i. flattery
10. statue	j. something that completes

For more on easily confused words and how to tell them apart, see Chapter 7.

X. Spelling

English is a very difficult language to spell correctly, since so many words in this language come from such a wide variety of other languages. Here are some words that are often misspelled. Mark them *C* if they are correctly spelled or *I* if they are incorrectly spelled.

1. mispell
2. acommodate
3. reccommend
4. misapply
5. disservice
6. hopeing
7. dissappoint
8. ellaborate
9. collaborate
10. stopped

Check your answers on page 24. For more spelling hints, see Chapter 9.

Answers To Quizzes

Remember, these quizzes are just to help you figure out your strengths and weaknesses, and to help you learn a few more words. Try taking them again after you have looked up some words in the dictionary, read this book, or just done a little more reading. You'll be surprised at how much more you've learned!

I. Difficult Words

1. a	2. c	3. b	4. a
5. a	6. b	7. c	8. b
9. a	10. a		

II. Words in Context

1. c	2. a	3. c	4. b
5. b	6. a	7. c	8. a
9. c	10. b		

III. Greek and Latin Roots

1. a	2. c	3. a	4. c
5. b	6. c	7. b	8. c
9. a	10. a		

IV. Prefixes

1. g	2. h	3. j	4. i
5. b	6. d	7. c	8. a
9. f	10. e		

V. Word Groups

1. f	2. g	3. j	4. h
5. i	6. b	7. a	8. c
9. e	10. d		

VI. Synonyms and Antonyms

1. a	2. c	3. b	4. a
5. a	6. b	7. c	8. a
9. c	10. a		

VII. Word Histories

1. c	2. c	3. a	4. b
5. b	6. c	7. a	8. b
9. a	10. b		

VIII. Words From Foreign Languages

1. b	2. j	3. f	4. g
5. c	6. d	7. e, h	8. e, h
9. i	10. a		

IX. Words Often Confused

1. f	2. e	3. g	4. h
5. j	6. i	7. b	8. a
9. c	10. d		

X. Spelling

1. I—misspell	6. I—hoping
2. I—accommodate	7. I—disappoint
3. I—recommend	8. I—elaborate
4. C	9. C
5. C	10. C

Chapter 1:
Aids to Building a Better Vocabulary
(Vocabulary Secrets Revealed!)

Building a vocabulary isn't something that you work on for ten minutes a day and then forget about. It's a process that is part of your reading, speaking, and writing every day. Each time you come across a word that you don't understand but look up, each time you search for a word that would express just exactly what you mean, each time you figure out a word from its context—you are building your vocabulary.

You don't have to engage in this process alone. There are several books that can help, and there are various ways you can stretch your memory to help you hold onto new words and their meanings.

Books That Help Build Vocabulary
(Read All About It!)

There are several types of books that can help you extend your vocabulary. They include:

Dictionaries

A *dictionary* lists words and their definitions. It usually has a guide to pronunciation too. When there is more than one way to pronounce a word, a dictionary tells you which way is "preferred," or

25

whether one or more pronunciations are equally acceptable. A dictionary also lists several meanings of a word, including meanings that the word used to have, or *archaic* (old-fashioned and obsolete) meanings. Dictionaries may give example sentences to show you how a word can be used. Some dictionaries list synonyms and antonyms for certain words.

In order to make the best use of dictionaries, you should understand all of their symbols and abbreviations. To save space, many dictionaries use abbreviations like *ant.* for *antonym* or *arch.* for *archaic*. Most dictionaries have guides to these abbreviations in the front or back. Likewise, you can find explanations of their pronunciation guides in the front, the back, or sometimes running along the top or bottom of each page. Once in a while, when you are looking up a word, take a few extra minutes to leaf through the dictionary you are using. Some dictionaries have sections where they define names, list geographical locations, and provide historical information and other useful facts. The more you know about your dictionary, the better use you can make of it.

What's the best way to use a dictionary to build vocabulary? Obviously, you can use a dictionary to look up any word you don't know. That's the easiest way to be sure you've understood the word's exact meaning. But you can also use a dictionary to check the meaning of a word you're not sure about. When you are writing, for example, you might check out just what a confusing or unusual word means in order to be sure you're using it the right way. Dictionaries that give example sentences are especially useful for this.

You can also use a dictionary to check the pronunciation of a word that you've seen but not heard.

Oxford English Dictionary. This special dictionary has more information than you will need for everyday use, but it can be a fun place for finding out more about words, their roots, and their histories. The *Oxford English Dictionary* contains a complete history of each word in the English language: when it was first used, what it used to mean, how its meaning has changed, and how it is used now. If you are interested in having fun with words, you might check out a few definitions in your library's copy of the *O.E.D.*

Dictionary of Synonyms and Antonyms. This specialized dictionary is just what its name suggests: it specializes in giving synonyms and antonyms. Usually it only lists these words, rather than explaining the shades of difference between their meanings. It can be helpful for locating a word that you understand but just can't remember; it is less helpful for learning new words, since it doesn't explain these words' meanings.

Rhyming Dictionary. Many poets use rhyming dictionaries to help them find rhymes. If you are interested in memorizing lots of new words, you might use a rhyming dictionary to help your memory. Writing yourself a rhyme or memorizing words in rhyming groups (*refrain, arraign; disdain, demesne*) can be easier than remembering random lists.

Thesaurus

This useful book may give you the most help in building a vocabulary. At its simplest, a thesaurus lists several synonyms for the words it contains.

Some thesauruses list antonyms as well. If you are searching for a word that you can't quite remember, a thesaurus will help you find it. If you are looking to build your vocabulary, you might combine the use of a thesaurus and a dictionary, looking up words in the thesaurus and then pinning down their meanings with the help of a dictionary.

Memory Tricks and Aids (Remember This!)

Once you've looked up a word or discovered its meaning in some other way, you're able to go on reading the passage where you discovered the new word. However, you might stop a minute and think of a way to remember the new word and its meaning. Devices that help your memory are called *mnemonic* devices. Here are a few that might help you:

Puns and Plays on Letters

Of course, you know the most common meaning of the words *bulls* and *bears*; but did you know that these words are also used to describe different types of buyers in the stock market? *Bulls* are the traders who think the market will go up; *bears* are the traders who are more pessimistic and think the market will go down. How could you remember which is which? Here is a mnemonic device that can help:

Bulls think the market will go up.
Bear down!

The play on the letter u can help you remember the meaning of the word bull. And the catch phrase Bear down! can help you recall what bears do.

Likewise, do you know the difference between *stalactites* and *stalagmites*? Both are deposits that are found in caves. They look like icicles, but they are made of stone. A stalactite hangs from the ceiling of a cave; a stalagmite "grows" up from the cave's floor. How could you remember which is which?

Stalactites hang from the ceiling.
Stalagmites grow from the ground.

Mnemonic Sentences

Write yourself a sentence that explains the meaning of the word, so that if you remember the sentence, you can remember the word. What's the advantage of writing a "memory sentence" instead of just memorizing a definition? A sentence can also tell a story or make a little picture in your mind. If you can associate a new word with a picture or an image, you strengthen your memory more than if you simply associated the new word with other words. For example, the word *vivacious* means "lively" or "spirited." Say you wrote the following sentence to help you remember that word:

Vivacious Vivian is very lively.

So far, so good. If you can remember the sentence, you will remember that *vivacious* means "lively." How can you remember the sentence? Use pictures and images to help you. As you think the word *vivacious*, picture a lively girl named Vivian. What is she doing? What color is her hair? What kind of clothes is she wearing? This mental picture will help you remember the sentence, which in turn will help you remember the definition of the new word.

Chapter 2:
Prefixes (First Things First)

A prefix is a part of a word that comes *before*. For example, in the following list of words, the prefixes are all underlined:

<u>under</u>line
<u>under</u>take
<u>under</u>stand
<u>under</u>go
<u>under</u>write

The prefix *under-* is a word part that comes before the rest of the word and affects its meaning.

Sometimes a prefix is a word part that doesn't make any sense on its own:

<u>pre</u>view
<u>pre</u>fix
<u>pre</u>test
<u>pre</u>pare
<u>pre</u>dict

The prefix *pre-* comes from a Latin word that means ''before,'' so that all of the above words include the idea of *before* in their meaning. To *preview* something is to look at it *before* someone else sees it, or before you've had a chance to look at it carefully. A *prefix* is a word part that comes before the rest of the word.

You take a *pretest* before you study a lesson, and you *prepare* for the test before you take it. It helps you *predict* your work; that is, to know something about your work ahead of time.

As you can see, knowing the meaning of a prefix can help you both to understand a word better and to remember it. If you know that the prefix *pre-* means "before," you've already got a head start on remembering the meaning of the word *preclude,* which means "to make impossible in advance, or before":

> Sinkerville High School's swim team lost
> yesterday's meet, which *precludes* any
> chance of going to the state finals.

Most prefixes come from Greek and Latin. The more prefixes you recognize and understand, the more quickly you can build your vocabulary. You will have an easier time both recognizing and understanding new words, based on your knowledge of their prefixes.

There are many different types of prefixes.

Prefixes That Give Numbers (You Can Count on These!)

Do you know the difference between a *unicycle,* a *bicycle,* and a *tricycle?* If you do, it's only because you recognize the difference between the prefixes *uni-, bi-,* and *tri-. Uni-* means "one," and a unicycle has only one wheel. *Bi-* means "two," and a bicycle has two wheels. *Tri-* means "three," and a tricycle has three wheels. Here are some more examples of the *uni-, bi-,* and *tri-* prefixes, plus other prefixes and words that go with them.

Uni- means "one." It comes from Latin.

> ▶ *unanimous*—of *one* mind, or in complete agreement.

The decision of the meeting was *unanimous.* Everyone voted to hire The Squealers to play at the dance.

> ▶ *uniform*—of *one* form. A *uniform* is also a kind of clothing that is the same for everyone.

The students at my school must wear a *uniform.* Everyone wears a gray jacket and dark blue pants.

> When something is *uniform,* it is the same for everyone.

The principal decided to have *uniform* standards for all written tests. Every question on each test had to meet certain standards.

> ▶ *unify*—to *unify* a group of things or people is to combine it into *one.*

After the Revolutionary War, the thirteen colonies were *unified* into one nation.

> ▶ *unite*—to *unite* is to join with others to make a whole.

The United States and the Soviet Union *united* to fight Hitler in World War II.

As you can see, *unify* and *unite* are quite similar in meaning. That is because they have the same prefix, *uni-.* *Unite* carries more the sense of *join,* focusing on the idea of many different parts or people joining together. *Unify* conveys the idea of making one whole entity, so unified that you can no longer tell one part from the next. Two countries *unite* to form an alliance, but each country keeps its separate identity. Many colonies are *unified* into one nation because each colony loses its separate identity to become part of a whole.

▶ *unique*—the *one* and only; having no equal. That hair style is *unique*! I've certainly never seen one like it on anyone else!

Do you know what a *unicorn* is?
  Hint: You already know the meaning of the prefix *uni-*. The word part *corn* comes from a Latin word meaning "horn."

Mono- also means "one." It comes from the Greek.

▶ *monocle*—a type of eyeglass that has only *one* lens.
Lord Basil raised the *monocle* to his left eye and looked sharply at his butler.

▶ *monologue*—a long speech by one person. The word comes from the theater, in which an actor might speak a long *monologue* while another actor listens quietly. However, the word can also be used to describe such a speech by a person off the stage.
Wendy Windjammer's *monologue* about her trip to India was interesting, but I wish that she hadn't talked so long.

▶ *monopoly*—*one* company that is the only company to make or sell a certain product. To have a *monopoly* means to be the one person or company to own something.

Politicians in the nineteenth century were concerned about *monopolies*. They were afraid that if one company owned all of one kind of product, that *monopoly* could raise its prices. At that time, Standard Oil almost had a *monopoly* on the nation's oil.

► *monotone*—A *monotone* is *one* tone.
► *monotonous*—something that is *monotonous* stays on the same tone, or subject, and is therefore very boring.

Mona spoke in a *monotone*, with almost no expression in her voice. It became *monotonous* to listen to her, although she is usually not *monotonous*, but very interesting.

Can you guess what a *monogram* is?

mono = one   *gram* = letter

When two or more letters are combined into *one* design, that is called a *monogram*.

Bi- means "two." This prefix is often used to describe different periods of time.

► *biweekly*—once every *two* weeks[1].
► *bimonthly*—once every *two* months.
► *biannual*—*two* times a year.
► *biennial*—every *two* years.

The *biweekly* magazine will not be on the newsstand until next week.

Our *bimonthly* meetings will be held in February and April.

The Horse and Buggy Club gives a *biannual* dance every winter and summer to raise money.

---

[1] *Semiweekly* and *semimonthly* should be used when the meaning is twice a week and twice a month.

34

I'm glad my birthday is an annual event and not a *biennial* one!

> ▶ *biceps*—*Biceps* are the large muscles in the front of the upper arm or at the back of the thigh.

Years of training helped the weightlifter develop powerful *biceps* which stood out impressively when he flexed his arms.

Tri- means "three." You may already know several words that use this prefix.

A *triangle* has *three* angles and three sides.

A *trio* is a group of *three*.

Triplets come in *threes,* whether you're talking about *three* children born at the same time or *three* notes in music played together.

Quart- means "fourth."

A *quarter* of something is *one-fourth* of it.

Twenty-five cents is one *quarter* of a dollar.

A *quart* is one-fourth of a gallon.

A *quartet* is four players in a musical group.

Can you guess the meanings of the following words? Just start counting!

quintet, sextet, septet, octet

Some other number prefixes:

A <u>penta</u>gon has *five* sides; an <u>octa</u>gon has *eight* sides.

A <u>dec</u>ade is a *ten*-year period.

A <u>dec</u>asyllable is a line of poetry having *ten* syllables.

Here is a chart of how to count by prefixes:

1—	*uni-* *mono-*	6—	*ses-* *sex-*
2—	*bi-*	7—	*sept-*
3—	*tri-*	8—	*oct-*
4—	*quart-* *quadri-*	9—	*non-* *nov-*
5—	*penta-* *quin-*	10—	*dec-*

Prefixes That Give Descriptions
(What Kind Is It?)

Some prefixes help you understand more about the *quality* of the word of which they are a part. For example, a *microscope* is something that helps you look at very small items, items that are too small to be visible to the naked eye.

> Hortense used her *microscope* to look at the blood cells.

The prefix *micro-* means "small."

A *benefactor* is someone who does a good deed for someone else.

> Mr. Midas has been my *benefactor*; he gave me the money to go to college.

The prefix *bene-* means "well" or "good." As you can see, knowing the meaning of the prefix helps you to understand and remember the meaning of a word.

Here are some prefixes that tell about the quality of something, along with some words that use these prefixes:

Bene- means "well" or "good."

36

► *beneficiary*—someone who receives a *benefit*.
(Can you recognize the prefix in
the word *benefit*?)

I was the *beneficiary* of Mr. Midas's good will.

► *benevolent*—the quality of *good* will and
generosity.

Pablo smiled at his friends in a *benevolent* way.

The *benevolent* man forgave the children who broke
his window.

► *benign*—good-natured, or kindly. In medical
terms, something *benign* is something that does no harm.

Rodney Rodriguez was in a *benign* mood, so he
decided not to send back his scrambled eggs, even
though he had ordered them sunny-side up.

Mal- on the other hand, means "evil" or "bad."

► *malcontent*—someone who is never happy.

The *malcontent* complained loudly to the waitress,
even though she had done everything perfectly as
far as I could see.

► *maladroit*—clumsy. *Adroit* means graceful, skill-
ful, or nimble, so *maladroit* means
the opposite.

Klutzy Clarence cleaned up the broken dishes in a
maladroit fashion, nearly cutting himself on the sharp
glass. Then he *adroitly* straightened the tablecloth,
so you could not tell that there had been an accident.

► *malaise*—a vague feeling of discomfort.
From *mal* and *aise*, a French word
meaning "ease." *Malaise* is the lack
of ease.

Mallory had a slight headache and sore throat. Gradually she became aware of her growing *malaise*.

Can you guess what the word *maladjusted* means?

> If someone who is well adjusted fits in well with the environment, what might someone who is *maladjusted* be like?

Neo- means "new."
► *neophyte*—someone who is *new* at something. Wanda is an experienced swimmer, but she was a *neophyte* on the basketball court.

Sometimes the prefix *neo-* will be added to a historical or artistic period. This is used to refer to a later, or newer, version of the original style.

> The Greeks invented the *classical* style.

> Ever since the Greeks, many architects have used a *neoclassical* style.

Semi- means "half."
► *semicircle*—a *half* circle.
We sat in a *semicircle* around the speaker.

Sometimes the prefix *semi-* will be added to a word to show that the word is only partly true.

> Angelo Adrenaline sat up straight, fully *conscious* of the danger.

> Sophia Siesta had been sleeping all afternoon and even now was in a *semiconscious* state. She had not fully awakened from her long nap.

Pseudo- means "false."

► *pseudonym*—a *false* name.

"Mark Twain" is a *pseudonym* for Samuel Langhorne Clemens.

The criminal was using a *pseudonym*, but the detective recognized him anyway.

Sometimes the prefix *pseudo-* will be added to a word to show that something is false.

> Astronomy is a *science*.
> Many people consider astrology a *pseudoscience*, or false science (i.e., something that pretends to be a science).

Micro- means "small."

► *microcosm*—a *small* world or miniature universe.

In this terrarium, we can see a *microcosm* of a rain forest.

► *microfilm*—film on which documents are printed in reduced, or *small*, form.

Use this machine to enlarge the print on that *microfilm*.

Scientists often add the prefix *micro-* to a word to show that it concerns very small degrees. A *microsecond* is a tiny fraction of a second. A *microphotograph* is a very small photograph that must be enlarged for the details to be visible. A *microdot* is used by spies. It is a tiny dot, the size of a pinhead, that contains a document or list that has been reduced to miniature size. A microdot can be hidden inside the period on an ordinary letter, for instance.

The opposite of *micro-* is *macro-*, which means "big." This prefix is mainly used in scientific terms;

but if you ever run into it, you will know that the word refers to the big picture. *Macroeconomics*, for example, is the study of the entire economic system, whereas *microeconomics* is the study of a tiny unit, such as one factory. *Macrobiotic* cooking looks at the big picture, i.e., how each part of a diet fits into the whole diet.

If a *microcosm* is a tiny world, can you guess what a *macrocosm* is?

Omni- means "all."
> ► *omnipotent*—An *omnipotent* person is *all-powerful*. *Omnipotence* means "total power."

The *omnipotent* king could not be challenged or contradicted by anyone. His *omnipotence* extended throughout his realm.

Multi- means "many."
> ► *multitude*—a large number; a crowd; *many* people or things.

Flora opened her window and was surprised at the *multitude* of flowers growing below.

The *multitude* gathered on the hillside, screaming loudly for justice.

> ► *multiply*—to make *many* out of one.

The number of people attending the dance *multiplied* so fast that we had to find more space.

Sometimes the prefix *multi-* will be added to a word to show that there are many of something.

In the first *stage,* the rocket will go through
the atmosphere. This will be a *multistage*
takeoff; I believe the rocket has at least three
stages.

This room has only one *purpose;* the *multipurpose*
room is over there.

Prefixes That Come From Prepositions
(A New Point of View)

Many prefixes come from words that were once
prepositions; that is, words that expressed a
direction or a position. For example, the prefix *super-*
means "over" or "above." The word *supervise*
literally means "to oversee" or "to manage" something or someone.

Will you *supervise* the arrangements for the
band if I *supervise* the sale of the dance tickets?

Knowing the meaning of prefixes that used to be
prepositions can help you to understand, recognize,
and remember the words that use them. A preposi-
tional prefix often gives a "feel" for the meaning of
a word, even if the prefix no longer shows its literal
meaning. For example, the prefix *trans-* means
"across" or "through." To *transpose* means "to shift
something out of its original position into a new
position." You can still "feel" the original meaning
of *trans*—to *transpose* something is to move it
"across," or "through," a space. But the current
meaning of the word focuses less on moving something through space and more on rearranging or
changing its position.

When spelling the word *receive,* Jana
accidentally *transposed* the *e* and the *i,*
so that the word came out *recieve.*

Here are some prefixes that come from prepositions, and some words that use these prefixes (keep an eye out for which words use the original meanings of the prepositions and which ones have changed the meanings slightly):

A- or *an-* means "without."

▶ *amoral—without* morality. Notice the difference between this word and *immoral,* which means something that breaks the rules, something that goes *against* morality.

An *amoral* person is not even conscious of the idea of right and wrong.

▶ *anarchy—without* a ruler; the complete absence of government; disorder and lawlessness.

When Ms. D. Meanor returned to her classroom, she found complete *anarchy:* some of the students were playing music, others were dancing, and still others were eating their lunch.

Do you know some other "archy" words? The root *arch* comes from the Greek word *archos,* meaning "ruler."

patriarch—a father *ruler.*

matriarch—a mother *ruler.*

monarch—a single *ruler,* such as a king or queen. (Did you recognize the prefix *mono*?)

hierarchy—a system of *rulers,* a way of arranging *rulers* by rank, from the lowest to the highest.

oligarchy—a system of government in which a very few people are the *rulers.*

A- or *ab-* means "from."

► *absolve*—to pronounce free *from* blame or
       responsibility.

After the judge heard the story, she *absolved* the
defendant of all responsibility for the accident.

► *absorb*—to suck up or drink in (to drink in *from*
       somewhere); to take up fully the
       time or attention of someone; to take
       in information and understand it.

Will those paper towels *absorb* that coffee you spilled?

Juan was fully *absorbed* in his duties as team captain.

Have you *absorbed* this information, or should we go
over it again?

► *abstain*—to hold back *from*, voluntarily to do
       without.

Dee Fault *abstained* from voting because she could
not choose between the two candidates.

► *abstinence*—voluntarily staying away *from*
       something; the act of abstaining.

Abstinence from smoking is good for your health.

► *abstract*—thought that is apart *from* any particular
       detail; thought that is not concrete.

The candidate's ideas for ending pollution are a little
abstract. They sound good in theory, but I'm not sure
they would work in practice. He discussed only
abstract ideas, without giving us any concrete
examples.

A- or *ad-* means "to." Be careful! Sometimes the
prefixes *an-*, *ab-*, and *ad-* all get shortened to *a-* to
make the word easier to pronounce. You can't

always tell just from looking at a word whether the *a-* means ''without,'' ''from,'' or ''to.'' However, once you know, you can usually remember; and this helps you to remember the meaning of the word.

▶ *accede*—to enter *into* the duties of an office; to agree *to*.

Camilla *acceded* to the office of class president yesterday.

The class *acceded* to the new rules for holding dances.

▶ *acquiesce*—to agree *to*, to go along with, often reluctantly.

If you want to hire that new band, I will *acquiesce*, although I prefer the band we hired last year. After a long argument, Mr. Gardner *acquiesced* to the idea of using his back yard for the block party.

▶ *acquire*—to get or to gain by one's own efforts (to bring something *to* yourself).

Sylvester finally *acquired* enough money to buy those tickets.

After many years, David Copperfield *acquired* the education he sought.

▶ *acquit*—to release someone from a duty or to clear someone from an accusation (to bring quiet *to* the person).

I will *acquit* you of your duties in the garden if you promise to do the dishes and sweep the floor.

The prisoner was *acquitted* of all charges and allowed to go free.

▶ *adjust*—to change so as to fit *into* something.

Thaddeus has not yet *adjusted* to his new school; he keeps expecting the gym to be where the library is!

Anti- means "against."

► *anticlimax*—a sudden drop from something important into something much less important (something that goes *against* the climax, or peak).

After Marc told me that he had won a four-year scholarship to college, it was certainly an *anticlimax* to hear him say that he also won free French fries at the fast food store.

That movie was great, but it was a real *anticlimax* to have to watch the hero getting married. I thought the movie should have ended as soon as he and the heroine escaped from the snake pit.

► *antidote*—a cure that works *against* a poison or some other bad thing.

The prospector searched frantically for the *antidote* to a rattlesnake bite.

The *antidote* to your blues is a day in the country; let's go for a drive!

► *antipathy*—a hostile feeling *against* someone or something.

Rex has an *antipathy* for romantic movies; he only likes adventure stories.

Note: Don't confuse *anti-*, which means "against," with *ante-*, which means "before." It's easy to get confused, because *ante-* is sometimes spelled with an *i:*

> *antipasto*—a salad or other food eaten *before* the pasta.

> *anticipate*—expecting something *before* it happens.

Vinnie did not *anticipate* winning a free *antipasto!*

Sheila Proove *anticipated* a delightful evening at the new Italian restaurant!

Sometimes the prefix *anti-* is added to a word to indicate the opposite of that word.

> *Matter* is the material from which the universe is made.

> *Antimatter* is the exact opposite of matter.

Com- or *con-* means "with."

► *concede*—to admit as true (to go along *with*).

After hours of arguing, Veronica finally *conceded* that Betty had a point.

► *conclude*—to bring to a close (to finish *with*).

The concert *concluded* with a medley of Beatles songs.
How shall I *conclude* my speech? Should I end with a joke, or would it be better to sound serious?

► *compare*—to examine in order to find similarities and differences (to make equal *with* something in order to see where the differences are).

You can't *compare* apples and oranges!
When you *compare* my work to Bill's, you'll see that he is good at languages and I am good at math.

► *compel*—to force to do something (to drive someone along *with* you).

If you will not follow the rules voluntarily, the vice-principal will *compel* you to obey by force.

The monarch *compelled* her subjects to pay high taxes.

▶ *compete*—to be rivals *with*, to be in contest *with*. "I will not *compete* with you for the coach's attention," said Melba. "She must notice me on her own."

Our team will *compete* at the state finals next week.

Do you know other words that come from *compete*?

competition—a contest; a place where people compete; the act of competing.

Are you entering the *competition* for best tennis player, or are you staying on the sidelines?

I am staying on the sidelines; too much *competition* makes me uncomfortable.

competitive—describes someone who likes to compete or someone or something that competes well.

Ginny is very *competitive*. She is always comparing herself to others to see who comes out ahead.

This new sports car is a very *competitive* model and should do well in today's market.

▶ *competent*—describes someone who is well qualified and capable.

Julio is a very *competent* doctor; all of his patients are doing very well.

Are you *competent* to drive this car, or should I find someone who has had more experience with a stick shift?

► *comprehend*—to understand; to go along *with* mentally; to include *with*.

The jazz musician could easily *comprehend* how the new melody changed the song.

The service charge is *comprehended* in the price.

► *comprehensive*—dealing *with* all or many important details; including everything *with* it.

This book report is quite *comprehensive*; Philip felt that he had learned everything he needed to know from it.

That is a *comprehensive* price; it includes airfare, hotel charges, and the taxi service from the airport.

Contra- means ''against'' or ''opposed to.''

► *contradict*—to speak *against* someone or something; to assert the opposite of what someone has said or to deny it.

When Mario said that Maria was late, she *contradicted* him by insisting that she had been on time. In her opinion, *he* was *early!*

► *contrary*—*opposed*, in opposition to, or different; unfavorable.

Do I want to go to the concert? On the *contrary*, I wouldn't go if you paid me!

Horace the horse had a *contrary* disposition; whatever his master wanted, the horse did the opposite.

► *contrast*—to compare so as to point out the differences; to make something clear by *opposing* it to something else; a sharp difference.

48

The light blue *contrasts* nicely with that dark green.

The baby is sleeping quietly. What a *contrast* to her behavior last night!

▶ *contravene*—to go *against*; to conflict with; to violate.

The disobedient servant *contravened* the wishes of the king.

▶ *controversy*—discussion of a question in which *opposing* opinions clash.

We had quite a *controversy* yesterday over whether team members should be allowed to attend games for free.

Something *controversial* involves a controversy.
Chewing gum in school is quite a *controversial* subject. Some people think it should be allowed; others are against it.

De- means "from."

▶ *deduce*—to come to a conclusion *from* certain facts; to bring a conclusion out *from* various facts.

Sherlock Catnip saw the spilled milk, heard the screen door slam, and could see tiny footprints on the floor. From this he *deduced* that his cat had overturned its dish and run outside.

▶ *defect*—the lack of something necessary; a shortcoming. (This is one of those words where it is difficult to come up with an exact translation of the prefix.)

The plan had a serious *defect*: it did not explain what we should do if we ran out of money.

Defect can also be a verb: to leave an organization or a cause, sometimes to join the opposition.

> Benedict Arnold *defected* from the American cause. He is one of the best known *defectors* in history.

Something that is *defective* has so many defects that it cannot be used, or else it has one serious defect.

> Bernard's plan is *defective*: it does not explain how we will raise the money we need.

> Bernadette's plan is *defective* in one major area: it does not explain what happens if the money runs out.

▶ *defer*—to put off (*from* this time) to a future time; to submit to the opinion of someone else.

We must *defer* our plans for the dance until we know whether the auditorium will be repaired.
If you think we can get the auditorium ready in time, I will *defer* to your judgment.

▶ *dejected*—in low spirits; depressed (cast down *from* good spirits).

Seymour was greatly *dejected* after losing the game.

▶ *delinquent*—failing to do what duty or the law requires.

"I would be *delinquent* in my duty," said Mr. Warner, "if I did not warn you that your project will be very difficult."

► *deprecate*—to feel and express disapproval of; to belittle.

Marcia *deprecated* the school team, saying that they had never won a game and were not likely to.

► *descend*—to come down *from*.

The princess slowly *descended* the long staircase, being careful not to trip on her dress as she walked down.

► *detour*—a turnoff *from* the most direct way.

This road is blocked off; we will have to take a *detour* to get to town.

► *detract*—to take away *from*; to make less good.

All the talking and shouting in the audience *detracted* from Beverly Bijou's enjoyment of the movie.

Don't confuse *detract* with *distract*. To *distract* someone is to draw his or her attention away from something.

The loud talking *distracted* Beverly, and she was not able to concentrate properly.

► *devious*—having moved away *from* the straight path, or from the honest way.

Our rivals took many *devious* twists and turns to reach their goal.

Joseph had a *devious* mind and seemed likely to trick his friend if she was not careful.

Ex- means "out of" or "from."

► *exaggerate*—to make something seem bigger or

more serious than it is (to go *out of* reality into another version of events).

Thomas always makes a mountain out of a molehill. I've never seen someone *exaggerate* the way he does!

▶ *exceed*—to go beyond a standard or a law (to go *out of* the normal or the legal into another state).

Marathon Marjory *exceeded* even her own best record in the race.

A careless driver may *exceed* the speed limit without even realizing it.

▶ *excel*—to be better than someone or something; to be especially good at something (to go *out of* the ordinary level of ability into a higher level).

Chester, the chess player, *excelled* at long periods of silent concentration.

Can you think of another word related to *excel*? You can? Excellent!

▶ *exempt*—to excuse or release someone; to free the person *from* a rule or condition that applies to others.

The queen *exempted* the poor subjects from paying their taxes because they had no money.

▶ *expose*—to show, *or* to leave open and unprotected, away *from* protection.

''I will *expose* you as a thief!'' shouted the detective.

► *extract*—to take out *from.*

Carefully the dentist *extracted* a tooth from her patient's mouth.

Inter- means "between."
> ► *intermediate*—a stage in the middle, *between* two others.

Lori could hardly wait to finish the *intermediate* grades and enter high school.

The boy's music lessons were at an *intermediate* stage: he was good enough to hit the right notes most of the time, but not good enough to play anything with feeling.

> ► *intervene*—to come *between* two people, places, or things.

Roy and Rosa wanted to continue their argument, but Mr. Rojas *intervened* and settled the fight.

Our track team would have won the meet, but fate *intervened:* our mascot ran out onto the field just as our star runner was about to take the lead!

Sometimes the prefix *inter-* is added to another word to give the sense of coming between.
> An *urban* system is a city system.
> An *interurban* system goes between cities.

Don't confuse *inter-* with *intra-. Intra-* carries the sense of "within" and "inside," whereas *inter-* carries the sense of "outside."
> An *intrastate* system stays inside the state.
> An *interstate* system goes outside the state, between two or more states.

Peri- means "around."

▶ *perimeter*—the border *around* something.
Can you measure the *perimeter* of this square?

▶ *periphery*—the area on the edge *around*
something.
Perry Winkle stayed on the *periphery* of the yard,
unwilling to come into the center.

▶ *periscope*—something that sees *around* things.
The submarine's *periscope* looked far out over the
water.

Pro- means "for" or "forward."

▶ *proceed*—to go on; to go *forward* with something.
Can we *proceed* with this meeting, or will there be
more delays?

Can you guess where the word *procession*
comes from?

Can you think of more words that come from
proceed?

proceedings—the results of a meeting.

processional—music to be played during
a procession.

procession—a march forward, or a group of
people marching forward.

process—a way of doing things; a development.

procedure—a particular way of doing things.

► *prominent*—sticking out; noticeable.

One of our most *prominent* lawyers, Ms. Sheila Case, will run for mayor.

The trophy was put in a *prominent* place on top of the bookcase.

► *promote*—to put *forward*, to advance to a higher position or to more attention.

The sergeant was *promoted* to captain because of his special bravery.

The movie studios are *promoting* this picture. They hope that if enough of us hear about it, we will all go to see it three or four times.

► *prosecute*—to bring the law against someone.

If you trespass into Mr. Grump's yard, he will *prosecute* you to get you to stop.

Sub- means "below" or "under."

► *subject*—As a verb, to put someone *under* someone or something else.

The prisoners were *subjected* to cruel treatment by the guards.

► *subject*—As an adjective, the state of being *under* someone or something else.

Tanya Hyde is *subject* to fits of temper.

► *subject*—As a noun, something that is *under* something else.

The *subjects* looked up as their king passed by.

Note: Of course, *subject* can also mean a course of study, as in school. As you can see, words take on many different meanings over the years.

► *subsequent*—coming afterwards; later.
Justin Time worried about being late to the meeting, but *subsequent* events showed him that he hadn't missed anything.

► *subside*—to settle down.
At first the crowd cheered wildly, but then the noise *subsided* and the crowd grew silent.

► *subsistence*—bare minimum needed for survival.
The peasants lived on a *subsistence* level, eating only what they could grow themselves.

Trans- means "across" or "through."

► *transact*—to carry a negotiation *through*.
We *transacted* our business quickly and efficiently.

► *transmit*—to send something *across* to.
Samuel Morse invented the Morse code in order to *transmit* messages by telegraph.

► *transparent*—able to be seen *through*.
The cloth was so thin and pale that it was almost as *transparent* as glass.

► *transport*—to carry something *across*.
Huge ships *transported* their cargo across the ocean.

► *transpose*—to move something into another place; to rearrange the order of something.
The printer had accidentally *transposed* those two letters and misspelled the word.

Chapter 3:
Roots (Can You Dig This?)

In Chapter 2 we saw how the prefixes at the beginnings of words could tell you something about their meanings. But what about the other word parts? A word's *root* is the main part of the word. Since English comes from many different languages, roots can come from many different languages as well. Many of the simplest words in the language have their roots in Anglo-Saxon or Middle English (spoken by people in England and Germany hundreds of years ago). Often, the more complicated English words have their roots in Latin (spoken by people in Italy and the Roman Empire over a thousand years ago).

These roots are the basic building blocks of many words. One root may be found in many different types of words, some of which are related and some of which are not. As with the prefixes, some words keep the original meaning of their root, whereas other words have moved further away from the original meaning of their root over the years.

Knowing about roots can help you build your vocabulary in two ways. As with prefixes, knowing a word's root can help you to remember and understand its meaning more easily. It can help you form a little picture in your mind of what the word means, because you will be able to recognize each part. As with prefixes, you can use the similarity among words with the same root to expand your vocabulary. It may be easier to learn and remember new words as part of a word group with the same root than simply as isolated words on a list.

Here are some basic roots that are often used in English, along with some of the many words that have grown from them. You may recognize some of these words from earlier chapters. Now you can build on both your knowledge of prefixes and on your memories of earlier words to cement the words you've already learned into your memory and to expand that knowledge to include related words:

The Latin word *dicere* means "to speak." One form of this word is *dict*.

▶ *predict*—*pre* = before; *dict* = say

   To *predict* something is to *say* something *before* it happens.

Claire Voyant *predicts* that the Mets will win the World Series again this year.

▶ *prediction*—The *-ion* ending (or *suffix*) tells you that this word is a noun. The rest of the word should tell you that it is related to *predict*. A *prediction* is something that has been *said before* it happens, something that has been predicted.

Will Claire's *prediction* about the Mets come true, or will some other team win?

▶ *addict*—*ad* = to; *dict* = say

   In Latin, this word means "to *say* yes

to'' or ''to agree to.'' In English, it has come to mean ''someone who has given himself or herself up to some strong habit,'' or ''to form some strong habit.''

Janet Java was *addicted* to coffee every morning; she couldn't wake up without it.

What can we do about the problem of drug *addicts* in our city?

▶ *addiction*—Again, the *-ion* ending tells you that this word is a noun, and the rest of the word tells you that it is related to *addict*. An *addiction* is the substance or habit to which an *addict* is *addicted*.

Lisa's only *addiction* was eating a piece of toast with strawberry jam each morning. If she could not keep up this habit, she felt that the whole day went wrong.

▶ *diction*—You can probably already guess something about the meaning of this word. The *dict* root tells you that it has something to do with speaking. The *-ion* ending tells you that it is a noun. *Diction* is the manner of speaking, either through the choice of words or through the way someone actually speaks.

I do not like that author's *diction*; his writing is too complicated and full of details for me.

▶ *dictum*—*Dictum* is something that has been said. It has come to mean a formal statement of opinion, or the handing down of a law.

Bernie the attorney objected to the judge's *dictum* that friends of the accused were not allowed in the courtroom.

So far, the words in this group have stayed fairly close to the meaning of their root, but there are some other words using this root that have slightly different meanings.

▶ *dictator*—The *-or* or *-er* ending should tell you that this word describes someone who does something. A buy*er* is someone who buys; a play*er* is someone who plays. A dictat*or* is someone who *dictates*, or who *says* how things ought to be. It has come to mean someone with absolute power to say how things ought to be.

The *dictator* ruled that no one could be on the streets after eight o'clock.

My new boss is a real *dictator*. She has to make every single decision herself and never listens to our opinions.

The word *dictate* has two meanings. One is the act of *saying* how something should be. However, you do not have to be a dictator to *dictate*.

The doctor *dictated* that the diet must be followed.

Of course, the other meaning of the word *dictate* is to *speak* words for someone else to write down.

I *dictated* the letter, and Terri wrote it down.

The word *dictation*—whose *-ion* ending should tell you that it is a noun related to *dictate*— is almost always used only with the second meaning of the word *dictate*. *Dictation* is what someone writes down when being *dictated* to, or the process of writing something down when being *dictated* to.

> Terri looked at the *dictation* she had taken, but she had written so quickly that she couldn't read a word.

> The lawyer's *dictation* went on for hours as his secretary struggled to take down the complicated directions.

Test yourself. Here are the words we have seen from the *dict* root. Do you remember their meanings? Do you at least have a "feel" for their meanings? Can you use your knowledge of roots and prefixes to jog your memory?

predict	dictator
prediction	dictate
addict	dictation
addiction	dictum
diction	

The Latin word *rogare* means "to ask."

▶ *interrogate—inter* = between; *rogate* = to ask

> To *interrogate* someone is *to ask* questions that go back and forth *between* two people. The word has come to mean "to ask questions formally of someone in order to find something out."

The police *interrogated* the witness for hours, but his story didn't change.

When Hamilton came home late last night, his parents began to *interrogate* him, but they soon learned that his car had had a flat tire.

▶ *interrogation*—The process of *interrogating* someone.

How long will this *interrogation* continue? I have an
appointment at the barber's!

▶ *derogatory*—The *-ory* ending should tell you that
this word is an adjective. The *rogat*
root should look familiar, and the
de- prefix may also look familiar.
(Did you remember that it means
"from"?) Unfortunately, this is one
of those words that can be related
to its original meaning but does not
follow the meaning of the word
parts exactly. Something *derogatory*
is something insulting or detracting.

Marisa made such *derogatory* comments about my
friend Brad that I decided not to ask her to my birthday party.

The *derogatory* article hurt the candidate's chances
for election by pointing out that the man had no
experience in office and seemed to have an unreliable
personality.

Even though you can't literally "translate" the roots
and suffixes of this word, nevertheless, you can see
how the meaning came about. *De-* means "from";
it also can mean "down from." Something derogatory carries the idea of saying (or *asking*) something
that brings someone "down from" a previously
good position.

▶ *arrogant*—This word comes from *ad-* meaning
"to," and *roga,* meaning "ask." The

-*ant* ending should tell you that it is an adjective. Again, we have to do a little detective work on this word: someone *arrogant* is someone who *asks* for too much power or brings too much power *to* himself or herself. To be *arrogant* is to be full of self-importance or haughty pride.

Hamilton is so *arrogant* that he actually thought I'd be honored to help him with his homework!

That movie star is never *arrogant*. He always seems just a little bit surprised at how successful he has become; in fact, he is quite humble.

Explore on your own
Here are some other *rogare* words. See if you can figure out their meanings or at least get a ''feel'' for them. Then check them out in your dictionary. Even if you don't memorize them this time around, you'll probably recognize at least some of them if you run across them in your reading.

> derogate
> arrogate
> abrogate
> arrogance

The Latin word *vita* means ''life,'' and the word *vivere* means ''to live.''

▶ *vital*—concerned with or relating to *life; or* full of *life; or* absolutely necessary (as if a matter of *life* and death).

The doctor checked the patient's *vital* signs to make sure the operation had been a success.

Juanita is one of the most *vital,* active people I know; she is always full of energy!

It is *vital* that these documents not fall into the wrong hands.

> ► *vitality*—The *-ity* ending should tell you that this is a noun. The rest of the word should tell you that this has something to do with *life* or with being *vital.* It means the power to live, or the quality of being "full of *life.*"

There is not much *vitality* left in these plants; you had better water them quickly!

Once Kay took over this club, its *vitality* returned and even increased.

> ► *vivid*—full of *life;* or bright and intense.

Dave wore a *vivid* shirt of bright blue; we could see him all the way down the block.

> ► *vivacious*—lively. The *-ious* ending should tell you that this word is an adjective. There is also a related adverb, *vivaciously.*

The *vivacious* hostess seemed to be everywhere at once, chatting, smiling, and serving food. She spoke so *vivaciously* that she made everyone with whom she spoke feel more lively.

Can you guess how the word *vitamin* got its name?

The Latin word *vincere* means "to conquer." The Latin word *victus* means "conquered."

► *victor*—The *-or* or *-er* ending tells you that this is someone who has done something. If a sell*er* is someone who sells and a dictat*or* is someone who dictates, what does a *victor* do? A victor *conquers.*

The *victor* of the track meet will receive a huge gold medal.

In the Civil War, it took many years of fighting before the North finally emerged as the *victor.*

► *victory*—what the victor has won; the fact of having *conquered.*

Victory on the football field is our coach's only thought.

"If I could finish writing this invitation," thought Victoria, "I would consider it a major *victory!*"

► *victorious*—Can you guess the meaning of this word? The *-ious* ending tells you that it is an adjective, and you already know that *victor* has something to do with conquering. A *victorious* person is someone who has *conquered,* or achieved *victory.*

The *victorious* players jumped up and down with excitement. At last they were the champions!

After Victor accepted her invitation to the dance, Victoria felt *victorious.*

► *convince*—The root *vince* comes from *vincere,* meaning "to conquer." The prefix *con-* means "with." To *convince* someone is to *conquer* them *with* your argument or ideas; that is, to bring them around to your point of view.

Percy Prunwell tried for hours to *convince* his parents to let him stay out until midnight. They were not *convinced* by his argument that all his friends stay out that late. What finally *convinced* them was his pointing out that he is a mature, responsible person who deserves to be trusted.

▶ *convict*—This word's history is related to *convince*, but, as with so many other words, the meaning has changed slightly. To *convict* someone is to prove that the person is guilty. You might say that you have *conquered* them *with* the evidence, or that you have *convinced* others—brought them along *with* you— to believe in the *convicted* person's guilt.

The prosecutor will try hard to *convict* the defendant, but his lawyer is *convinced* that the man is innocent.

"Let me explain why I broke our date," said Hope. "Do not *convict* me before you have heard me out!"

The word *convict* has also come to mean a person in jail; that is, someone who has been *convicted* of a crime.

▶ *conviction*—a firmly held belief; that is, a belief that has *conquered* you and brought you along *with* it. (Did the *-ion* ending clue you in on this word as a noun?) The word also means

> the attitude of firmly believing—or
> being *convinced*—by something.

It is my *conviction* that you should never start smoking. That way, you never have to worry about quitting.

Julie spoke with such *conviction* that Thomas almost believed her, but something in her manner told him he should doubt her.

Do you know the meaning of these *vict* words?
          evict   eviction
Clues: *e* or *ex* = out of
          ion = shows that the word is a noun
Make a guess if you don't know the words. Then look them up in your dictionary.

Finis in Latin means "end."

▶ *finish*—to *end* something.

▶ *final* — coming at the *end;* showing an ending.

"As soon as I *finish* the *final* page of this book," said Felix, "I'll start cooking dinner."

"I don't want lima beans for supper again tonight," said Oscar, "and that's *final!*"

▶ *finale*—the part of a program that comes at the *end*.

The magician pulled a rabbit out of a hat, sawed his assistant in half, and turned lead into gold. Then, for his grand *finale*, he disappeared in a puff of smoke.

▶ *finite*—having an *end*.

There are only a *finite* number of ways to solve this

problem. Soon you will learn them all.

My patience with you is *finite*—I will lose my temper soon!

> ► *infinite*—without an *end*. The prefix *in-* means, in this case, "not." Something that is *infinite* has no end or cannot be measured.

Writers have an *infinite* number of ways to end a story. I wonder how they ever choose?

The nurse showed *infinite* patience as he cared for the sick child.

Note: *Finite* and *infinite* are *antonyms;* that is, they have opposite meanings. For more information about synonyms and antonyms, see Chapter 4.

The list goes on....

finality	finalize	finally	finalist
infinitesimal	infinitely		

Guess the meanings of these *fin* words—or use your new knowledge of roots to figure out how these words got their meaning. If you have to look up a word that you don't know, look to see if your dictionary shows the origin of the word. You will probably find some version of *fin*.

Spectare is a Latin word meaning "to see."

> ► *suspect*—This word combines *sub-* ("under" or "beneath") with *spect* ("see"). To *suspect* something is to *see beneath* it, to have the idea that it is not the way

it seems on the surface, but hides a secret underneath.

Watson *suspected* that Shirley had not really forgotten to phone him. He *suspected* that she had simply not wanted to talk.

The police have *suspected* Mr. Stickyfingers for some time, but have never been able to prove that he was doing anything wrong.

> ► *spectacle*—a public display; something remarkable to *see*. The word *spectacle* can be either positive or negative in meaning, depending on how it is used.

The circus's trapeze act was incredible; it was a real *spectacle*!

Mark can be very immature at times. He made a *spectacle* of himself in the cafeteria today when he started a food fight.

> ► *perspective*—point of view. The *per-* prefix means "through," so in one way, the word can seem to mean *seeing through* something. A point of view can be a way of *seeing* something.

From my *perspective*, Dennis is wrong; but Dennis's own *perspective* is that he is right.

By the next day, I had gotten a little more *perspective* on the argument. I decided that we were both right.

> ► *circumspect*—an adjective meaning "careful" or "cautious." *Circum-* is a prefix meaning "around." Someone who is *circumspect* has looked all the way *around* something before speaking or acting.

You may ask Ms. Anne Thrope to lend us her best dishes, but be *circumspect*. Feel her out on the subject before you come right out and ask.

Words in context

If you know that the prefix *circum-* means "around," can you figure out the meanings of these words in context?

Christopher Columbus had hoped to *circumnavigate* the globe.

I will try to *circumvent* the rules, but I am not sure whether I can get around them.

What is the *circumference* of that circle?

Check your guesses in your dictionary.

▶ *inspect*—to look into, with the meaning of looking into very thoroughly.

Lucy *inspected* the fabric and decided that the dress was not worth the price on the tag.

The detective *inspected* the small shred of cloth, wondering if the tiny brown mark was a bloodstain or merely a spot of mud.

▶ *prospect*—If *pro-* means "forward" and *spect* means "see," wouldn't you guess that a *prospect* would have something to do with *looking forward*? A *prospect* is either something you *see* when you look *forward* or a place from which you can get a good *forward* view.

Bruno's *prospects* of going to college are excellent: he has good grades and lots of extracurricular activities.

70

The high mountain offered a beautiful *prospect* of the valley below.

Words in context

Can you figure out the meanings of these words?

Henry is a *prospective* world traveler: he has already started saving money for the trip.

The police *inspector* looked all over the factory, but he could not find any evidence that the fire had been planned. He decided to ask the fire department to conduct its own *inspection*.

Jacere is a Latin word meaning "to throw." In English, this root often takes the form of *ject*.

We already saw in Chapter 2 that *dejected* meant "depressed." Now we can see that it literally means "thrown from." Likewise, we saw that *subject* meant "under the rule of." Now we can see that it literally means "thrown under."

de = from	*ject* = throw
sub = under	*ject* = throw

Lonely and depressed, the *dejected* boy walked slowly down the street. He felt *subject* to a terrible mood of sadness. "Why must I be *subjected* to these terrible Friday quizzes?" he mumbled to himself. "Anyone would be *dejected* if he had to study as much as I do."

Then the boy decided to *reject* these depressing thoughts. How could he *inject* a little happiness into his life? He _projected_ for himself the image of how happy he would be on Saturday, once the test was over. His _rejection_ of gloomy thoughts helped to cheer him up. His _dejection_ was cured! Happily, he hurried home to begin a new _project._

Could you figure out the underlined words in the above paragraph, using their context and your knowledge of roots and prefixes?

Related words that you may have seen...

injection   projection   subjection

...And that you may not have seen:

abject   abjection   interject   interjection

When you look these words up, try looking up their origins as well. Most dictionaries give this information in parentheses right after the word itself. Remember that _ab-_ means "from" and _inter-_ means "between." See if you can relate the meanings to the origins.

Laborare is a Latin word meaning "to work."
▶ _labor_—either a verb meaning "to work very hard" or a noun meaning "work that is done."

Carmen _labored_ for hours over her term paper, but she was finally pleased with the results.
Raking leaves is a physical _labor_ Rocky enjoys, but taking exams is a mental _labor_ he doesn't enjoy.

A _laboratory_ is a place where _work_ is done. More specifically, it's a place where people experiment, trying out different things. It can be either an actual room or a situation.

> The scientist rushed back to her *laboratory* to check the results of her latest experiments.

> The softball team will be a kind of *laboratory*, where we can see which players stand up to pressure and which do not.

Do you remember the meaning of the prefix *con-*? It means "with." In the word *collaborate*, the *n* is turned into an *l* to make the word easier to pronounce. However, as you might guess, the word means "to work with."

> Smedley and I are *collaborating* on our science experiment. He dissects the frog, and I draw the diagrams.

> If the great nations of the world would *collaborate* on their space programs, we might make more progress.

Can you guess what a *collaborator* is? Did you remember that an *-or* ending means "the person who does something"? A *collaborator* is someone who *collaborates*.

> My *collaborator* and I are quite excited about our latest project. Together we are building a multistage rocket that will be able to fly to Jupiter.

Something that is *elaborate* has come *out of* (*e-* or *ex-*) a lot of *labor*. Something that is *elaborate* has been worked out in great detail—maybe too much detail.

Jessie came up with an *elaborate* plan for selling tickets to the dance. She wants us to sell tickets for $5.00 on Monday, $6.00 on Tuesday, and $10.00 on the day of the dance itself. I personally would prefer a simpler plan.

Elaborate can also be used as a verb, meaning "to go into more detail (to work something out further)."

"Jessie, I don't understand your plan. Perhaps you would *elaborate*. Tell us exactly what you think we should do."

More labor words

Can you guess the meaning of these words from context? Check your dictionary to see if you were right.

I understood you the first time; you don't need to *belabor* your point.

The tired man struggled *laboriously* up the hill, pausing at every step to catch his breath.

Chapter 4:
Synonyms and Antonyms
(Searching for Precise Meanings)

As we have learned, *synonyms* are words that are very similar to one another in meaning:

> pretty   beautiful   lovely   gorgeous

There are slight differences in meaning and in the "feel" of these words, but they all mean much the same thing. *Antonyms* are words that are opposed (*anti-*) to each other in meaning:

> pretty/ugly   high/low   fast/slow

One sure way of building your vocabulary is to look up words that interest you in a thesaurus. A thesaurus will give you many synonyms for a word. However, since each synonym has a slightly different meaning, you may not feel comfortable using it until you have run across it in your own reading. Do you remember the word game in the Introduction?

> I am *steady*.
> You are *calm*.
> He is *placid*.

These words are all synonyms, but each has a slightly different *connotation*, or suggestion. *Steady* suggests someone who is reliable, who is not easily shaken up by a bad situation and can be relied upon. *Calm* is not quite such a positive word. Someone who is *calm* is not upset, but perhaps this person is not quite as reliable as someone who is *steady*. *Placid* is a word that can be used to describe a cow peacefully munching grass in a field! *Placid* means "undisturbed." Yes, it also means "calm," but perhaps almost "too calm." This kind of calmness can come from being too complacent to get upset.

How can you avoid using the wrong synonym? Well, one answer is, you can't, so don't worry about it. Everyone makes mistakes in using words—that's part of writing and speaking, and it's nothing to be embarrassed about. However, it is true that the more you read, the more you will see how other people use words, and this will help give you a "feel" for all the shades of meaning that separate *placid* from *calm*. If you've looked up a word in your thesaurus, you'll at least have a general idea of its meaning. That should help you to gather the rest of its shades of meaning when you run across it in context.

Antonyms are a little easier. Some antonyms have clues right in their prefixes that they are the opposite of some other word. Other antonyms have clues in their roots that they oppose another word. On the other hand, some antonyms have no clues at all—but learning an antonym can help you become more precise about the meaning of two words at once: the word, and a word that is its antonym.

Antonyms With Clues in the Prefix
(Looking Up Front for Clues)

Here is a list of prefixes that in some way mean "not" or "bad":

in-   un-   anti-   mis-   dis-   non-

If these prefixes appear in front of a word, there is a good chance that the word is the antonym of its root word.

Appropriate—Inappropriate

Something that is *appropriate* matches or fits the situation. Something that is *inappropriate* does not fit the situation, and may even stand out because of that.

Kyle wore *appropriate* clothes to the wedding: a gray suit, a white shirt, and a dark red tie.

Gus wore *inappropriate* clothes to the wedding: a bright green clown suit with an orange wig and a false nose.

Would it be *appropriate* for me to invite Janey to our birthday party for Rae?

Janey and Rae are always fighting, so I think inviting Janey would be *inappropriate*.

Essential—Nonessential

Something that is *essential* is absolutely necessary. Something that is *nonessential* can easily be done without (or is *unnecessary*—another antonym!).

It is *essential* that we begin our hike at 5 A.M. Please take all *nonessential* items out of your backpack so that you do not carry any extra weight.

Frequent—Infrequent

Frequent means "often." *Infrequent* means "not very often."

Dr. Needlesticker's visits were quite *frequent*. When the patient was sick, the doctor came every day. Then the patient began to get better, and the doctor's visits grew more *infrequent*. Soon the doctor was coming only once every two weeks.

Adequate—Inadequate

If something is *adequate*, it is enough for the purposes it is being used for. Something that is *inadequate* cannot measure up to what is needed.

Will two cups of sugar be *adequate* for this cake, or do we need three?

The sales clerk, named Hy Price, said, "I am afraid that twenty dollars is *inadequate* for the purchase of this radio."

Trust—Mistrust

To *trust* someone means "to put your faith in that person, to believe that the person is reliable." To *mistrust* someone means "to believe that there is a strong chance of the person being unreliable." *Trust* and *mistrust* can also be used as nouns.

I *trust* Shari when she says she wants to help us, but I *mistrust* her when she says she has enough time. I *trust* her intentions, but I *mistrust* her actions.

Trust in your parents is important for good family relations. *Mistrust* between parents and children means that there will often be arguments.

Sometimes prefixes will show words that are antonyms by having opposite meanings themselves. For example, *pro-* means "forward" and *re-* means "backward."

Progress—Regress

To *progress* is to go forward. To *regress* is to go

backward. Usually these words are not used literally, but in a more general sense.

Pedro has *progressed* very well with his Spanish this summer, but Juanita seems to have forgotten everything she knew. I am afraid she has *regressed* a good deal.

Ascend—Descend

ascend = *ad* ''to'' + *scend* ''climb,''
      to go up or climb up.

descend = *de* ''down from'' + *scend* ''climb,''
      to go down or climb down.

Elly Vator quickly *ascended* the stairs to the second floor, but when she saw that her friend wasn't ready yet, she *descended* the stairs once more.

Our track team has quickly *ascended* to the semifinals. Our football team, however, has *descended* to last place.

Antonyms With Clues in the Root
(Digging Deeper for Clues)

You already know that *big* and *small* are antonyms. In Latin, *major* = big and *minor* = small. So *majority* and *minority* are antonyms.

majority—the most; more than 50 percent
      of a group.

minority—a small number, less than 50 percent
      of a group.

The *majority* of the class wanted to see a movie, but a *minority* voted to go on a nature walk instead.

Likewise, you already know that *most* and *least* are antonyms. In Latin, *maximum* = most and *minimum* = least.

When Amelia rented the airplane, she was told that she could use it for a *maximum* of two hours.

"In order to reach my destination," she protested, "I will require a *minimum* of three hours—I can't possibly fly there and back in less time than that!"

Related Words

maximum = the most
minimum = the least
optimum = the best

The *optimum* conditions for flying are a clear, sunny day and perhaps a breeze.

An *optimist* is a person who always sees the best in everything.

Antonyms That Have No Clues
(Are You Baffled by Mystery Meanings?)

It's true that there are many antonyms that you simply have to memorize, but each time you learn an antonym, remember that you are more than doubling your word power. Knowing a word along with its antonym helps you understand both words much better than knowing either word alone.

Attract—Repel

To *attract* something is to draw it closer.

To *repel* it is to push it further away.

One end of a magnet *attracts* other magnets; the other end *repels* them.

Olivia was *attracted* by the idea of going dancing, because she has always loved to dance. Reginald, however, was *repelled* by the idea. He hates loud music and crowds.

Deliberate—Accidental

Deliberate means "done on purpose."
Accidental means "done by accident."
These words also have adverb forms: *deliberately* and *accidentally*.

That was quite embarrassing when you suggested that Ms. Friztop should try your hairdresser. Was it *deliberate*?

No, it was *accidental!* How was I to know she had just had her hair done?

Slowly and *deliberately* the bank teller counted out the money. Nevertheless, she *accidentally* gave me an extra twenty dollars.

As you can see from the example, *deliberately* can also mean "with a lot of careful effort." In this sense, *deliberately* is not an antonym to *accidentally*, meaning "by accident."

Elevate—Lower

To *elevate* something is to raise it, or make it higher. To *lower* something is to bring it downward. *Elevate* may refer to things being actually lifted, or to raising the "tone" or "standard" of an idea or conversation.

The ballet dancer *elevated* his leg onto the bar and began to exercise. Slowly he *lowered* his head until he was bent in half.

Carrie always insists on talking about books and classical music, which gives her conversation a very *elevated* tone.

Eliminate—Restore

To *eliminate* something is to get rid of it. To *restore* something is to bring it back to its former state.

Archie Tecture, the architect, wants to *eliminate* these old wooden banisters and replace them with metal poles, but I would like to see the old wood fixed up and *restored* to its former state.

Last year our school *eliminated* its baseball team. This year there is more money in the budget and so the team has been *restored*.

Emerge—Recede

To *emerge* is to come out of something very slowly. To *recede* is to go back into something very slowly. (Did you notice that these antonyms have opposite prefixes, even though their roots are also different? *e* = out of; *re* = back to)

The swamp creature slowly *emerged* out of the muck, so that we saw first its ugly head, then its horrifying body, and finally its long, spiky tail.

Whenever there is a noisy crowd around, Prudence tends to *recede* into the background. I think she is quite shy.

Endure—Succumb

To *endure* is to last through something. To *succumb* is to give in.

The spy wondered if she could *endure* the horrible tortures. Would she *succumb* to the enemy and reveal all her secrets? Fortunately, she had *endured* worse than this! No, she would not *succumb;* she would never give in! She would find a way to escape!

Exaggerate—Minimize

To *exaggerate* something is to make it seem bigger than it is. To *minimize* something is to make it seem smaller than it is.

Leo always *exaggerates* his troubles. Every little thing is a major disaster to him.

Lila, on the other hand, *minimizes* her problems. She would have to be in real trouble before she asked anyone for help.

Institute—Abolish

To *institute* something is to start or establish it. To *abolish* something is to get rid of it.

Slavery was *instituted* in the New World when the slave trade began. It was *abolished* in the United States after the end of the Civil War.

Our gym teacher is *instituting* a new gymnastics program. Does this mean that our after-school gymnastics club will be *abolished?*

Praise—Condemn

To *praise* something is to say that it is good. To *condemn* something is to say that it is bad and perhaps that it should not even exist.

Our teacher *praised* good study habits and *condemned* poor ones.

Chapter 5:
Word Histories
(Meet Etta Mology)

By now you have probably begun to see that the more sharply you can form a picture in your mind to go with a word, the better you will remember the word. The more fun you have with a word, the more likely you are to remember it and to enjoy using it.

One way to form pictures that help you remember a word is through its history, or *etymology*. When you know where a word came from, you can use the story to help you remember what the word means today. Besides, word histories are fun! Here are some words and their histories:

▶ *amazon*—An *amazon* is a word that is used to describe a tall, strong woman. In Greek mythology, the *amazons* were a race of warrior women who fought with bows and arrows. In Shakespeare's play *A Midsummer Night's Dream*, the Greek king Theseus marries Hippolyta, queen of the amazons, but in other legends, amazon women never married.

Maxine Maximum strode like an *amazon* onto the basketball court.

▶ *boycott*—A *boycott* is a group decision to refuse to buy or do something as a form of protest. If a community did not like the activities of a certain company, for example, they could stage a *boycott*—everyone in the community would refuse to buy that company's products in order to force the company to change its activities. To *boycott* something is to act as a group in refusing to buy or do something.

The protesters decided to begin a *boycott* of Pox Box Company that would last until the company stopped polluting the local river. They asked citizens to *boycott* all Pox Box Company products. The protesters hoped that if no one bought Pox Box Company products, the company would change its actions.

The word *boycott* comes from Captain Charles *Boycott*, an Irish land agent who raised the rents of local farmers. Everyone in the community was so angry at Captain Boycott that they refused to associate with him—in effect, they *boycotted* him!

► *chauvinism*—This word means "extreme, blind patriotism or partiality to a cause, to such an extent that you look down with contempt on everyone who does not share your feelings."

Patriotism can be a good quality, but *chauvinism* can lead to wars or arguments between nations. A *chauvinist* believes that his or her group or cause is better than anyone else's, and that anyone of another group is a less valuable person.

The word comes from Nicholas *Chauvin*, a soldier in Napoleon's army who worshiped Napoleon as a hero who had no faults.

▶ *crestfallen*—Someone is *crestfallen* after a big disappointment. The word means "disappointed" or "dejected." A *crestfallen* person started out with high hopes but ran into trouble that caused disappointment. The word comes from the image of a rooster, whose *crest*—or crown—actually droops and *falls* after he loses a fight.

The *crestfallen* team returned to the clubhouse, wondering how they could have lost the big game, 10-0.

▶ *forum*—A *forum* is a place where public discussion can take place.

Our school newspaper can be a *forum* for student ideas.

In a regular newspaper, the letters to the editor column may be the *forum* for public opinion.

In ancient Rome, the marketplace at the center of the city was called the *forum*. Trials were held there, and often political speeches were made there as well. The Roman forums were the center of all kinds of activity for the towns.

▶ *galvanize*—To *galvanize* someone is to stir them into vigorous action. The word comes from Luigi *Galvani*, who studied electricity and was a professor in Bologna, Italy, in the eighteenth century. To *galvanize* someone is like stirring someone into action with an electric shock, with the word coming from Galvani's interest in electricity.

The speaker looked at the rows of bored students sitting in assembly. She smiled to herself as she thought of how her speech would *galvanize* them into action.

► *hackneyed*—This word means "cliched, boring, dull, overused." It is used in regard to words, expressions, and sometimes ideas.

Gigi's compositions were full of *hackneyed* expressions, like "neat as a pin" and "cute as a button."

The word comes from the carriage horses that came from *Hackney*, a part of the city of London. The *Hackney* horses tended to be old, worn-out, and broken-down. So a *hackneyed* expression is like a worn-out old horse—it's tired because it's been used too many times before.

► *lyrical*—*Lyrical* language is very musical language, as in poetry or very poetic prose. The word comes from the Greek instrument *lyre*, which was like a small harp. In Greek times, poets would strum on their lyres while reciting their poetry.

Do you like the *lyrical* speeches in *Romeo and Juliet,* or do you prefer the more modern love scenes in Woody Allen movies?

▶ *marathon*—A race that covers about twenty-six miles is called a *marathon.* Something that goes on for an extemely long time without stopping, often overnight, is also called a marathon.

The runners lined up for the start of the Boston *marathon.*

Last night at the office we had a *marathon* work session. We started at six o'clock, and we didn't finish until six the next morning.

The city of Marathon is about twenty-six miles away from Athens, the capital of Greece. In 490 B.C. some Athenians fought the Persians in a battle where the Athenians were outnumbered by ten to one—and won. A Greek ran the first *marathon* to bring the news to Athens.

▶ *maverick*—A *maverick* is someone who strikes out on his or her own, someone who doesn't follow the common herd. The word comes from Samuel A. *Maverick,* a Texas rancher of the 1840s who didn't brand his calves. The word used to mean "an unbranded calf," but came to mean "a person who wasn't 'branded'—that is, someone who didn't let another organization run his or her life.''

She is a real *maverick*—you can never tell what she's going to do next.

▶ *panacea*—A *panacea* can cure all ills. Often the word is used sarcastically to suggest that it is actually not possible to find something that will solve a problem so easily.

Mr. Bruce believes that hard work is the *panacea* for all of a person's problems.

The word comes from the name of one of the daughters of Asclepius, the Greek god of medicine. He named his daughter *Panakeia,* the all-healing. He meant the name in a positive way, but the word has taken on a somewhat negative tone.

▶ *sardonic*—This word means ''somewhat sarcastic'' or ''ironic.'' A *sardonic* smile has no laughter in it, but is rather a bitter or scornful smile.

''Oh, Stewart is definitely the best dancer,'' said Hugh with a *sardonic* smile as he watched Stewart trip over his partner's feet.

The word comes from the name of a poison plant growing on the island of Sardinia, with the Roman name of *herba Sardonia.* The Romans believed that this poisonous plant would cause the dying person's face to tighten up into what looked like a grim laugh—a sardonic smile.

► *Spartan*—A *Spartan* life is a plain and rugged life, with lots of exercise and no frills. *Spartan* in general means "difficult and plain."

We had a *Spartan* journey on the old train. There were no cushions on the seats and only a few old biscuits and some well water to drink.

The word comes from *Sparta*, a community of ancient Greece. The *Spartans* believed in living very simply, under rough conditions, and in training their young men to withstand pain and hardship.

► *tawdry*—*Tawdry* items are cheap and flashy. The word has a negative connotation, suggesting that the person who buys the tawdry item has very poor taste and is perhaps a bit showy and cheap.

The young starlet arrived for the audition dressed in a *tawdry* miniskirt that was supposed to look like real leather, but that looked more like some kind of cheap vinyl.

The word comes from the lace collars, named after *Saint Audrey*, that were sold at medieval fairs. When the quality of the lace went down, the collars were seen as cheap—and at the same time, their name was shortened to *t'Audrey*—or *tawdry*.

Chapter 6:
Foreign Words
(Hopscotching Around the World)

As we have seen, English comes from many different languages. Many English words come from Latin or Greek roots. Others come from Anglo-Saxon and Middle English—languages spoken in England and Germany hundreds of years ago. Many English words come from modern languages as well—French, German, Spanish, Italian, Arabic, and many others. These words and phrases make English a rich, interesting, and varied language.

Sometimes a foreign expression will be written in italics. When you use these expressions in your writing, you should underline them, just as you would underline the title of a book or movie. Putting foreign words in italics—or underlining them—shows that they are not really English. For example, a restaurant critic might write something like the following:

I loved Chez François's fabulous frogs' legs, which were cooked with a *soupçon* of garlic.

Soupçon is a French word that literally means "suspicion." In this case, it also means a "hint" or "tiny taste." Notice that when the word is put into italics, it has to be written with all the French accent marks that go with it.

Some words, however, have become so common in the English language that they are no longer put into italics. Different people follow different rules about this. Some people feel that every word that still sounds "foreign" should go into italics. Others feel that English has always assimilated, or absorbed, foreign words that are then no longer "foreign" but part of English.

You will have to decide for yourself, or with your teacher, which foreign words you think should be set off with italics and which should not. Most of the words on the list below have become so much a part of the English language that they are no longer put into italics. Some you may even recognize and you may be surprised to find that they were once part of another tongue!

► *aficionado*—This Spanish word means "someone who is a fan and perhaps a bit of an expert in a sport or an art."

Teddy is a real *aficionado* of folk dancing—he knows dances from fourteen different countries.

The football *aficionado* in our group is LaWanda—she can tell you anything you want to know about the game.

Hint: This word looks a little bit like the English word *affection*. An *aficionado* feels *affection* for a sport or an art.

► *apartheid*—This word comes from Afrikaans, a form of Dutch spoken by the descendants of Dutch settlers in South Africa. It refers to the policy of total segregation of white people from black people and people of other racial backgrounds.

Apartheid was instituted in South Africa after World War II when the South African government passed laws to separate people according to race.

> **Hint:** *Apartheid* contains the word *apart*, which can remind you that it is a policy of keeping races *apart*.

► *bodega*—A Spanish word that originally meant grocery store, wine shop, or wine cellar. *Bodega* in the United States has come to mean a little grocery store, especially one that sells Hispanic-American products.

Does the *bodega* on the corner sell garbanzo beans, or do we have to walk over to the supermarket?

> **Hint:** The word has a little bit of the same sound as *boutique*, which is the French word for "little shop." Both come from the Latin word *apotheca*, which in turn comes from the Greek *apotheke*, which comes from words that mean "to put away." A little shop is a place in which things are stored or put away.

► *bonanza*—This Spanish word originally meant a mine that had a good, rich vein of silver or gold in it. It was used in the Southwest United States, where there are gold and silver mines and where many Spanish words came into the language through Spanish and Mexican people. The word has eventually come to mean any lucky return on an investment, or just a good piece of luck.

I invested $5 in the Doggie Sweater and Jewelry Company, and it has turned out to be a real *bonanza*. The company was just bought up by a big toy company and my investment is now worth $500!

▶ *bravura*—*Bravura* is an Italian word that literally means "bravery." In English, it has come to mean "a brave show of spirit; something done with a lot of flash and style."

The rock star inwardly feared going out on stage, but when it was time for his entrance, he leapt on-stage with great *bravura*.

Hint: *Bravura* both means and sounds like *bravery*, although *bravura* suggests something slightly more than *bravery*.

▶ *cliché*—This word comes from French. Notice the accent over the *e*. It means "a stereotype" or "overly used idea."

Paul is always using *clichés*. Today he told me to "have a nice day," to "keep my chin up," and to "keep smiling."

Word History: The French took this word from the German *klitsch*, a clump or mass of clay. Originally clay was used to make patterns that could be used in printing. The French word *clicher* originally meant "to print from a metal printing plate." So something that is *clichéd* is as dull

94

and expected as something that has been printed out in hundreds of copies from the same printing plate.

▶ *dētente*—You've probably seen this word in the newspapers: it comes from the French, where it is related to the word meaning "relax" or "stretch out." A *dētente* is a relaxation, or easing up, of the strain between two governments.

The United States and the Soviet Union began a policy of *dētente* in the early 1970s. *Dētente* was supposed to bring about better relations between the two countries.

▶ *ersatz*—A word meaning "artificial" or "false," it comes from a German word that means "replacement." Something *ersatz* is a replacement, usually a replacement that is far worse than the thing it replaced.

Julie's eyes filled with tears, but I was sure that it was *ersatz* emotion and that she had no real reason to be sad.

▶ *faux pas*—These words are French meaning "false step." A *faux pas* is a social mistake, usually a comment or action that is accidentally insulting or inappropriate.

Boris made a real *faux pas* with Ms. Flopbottom. He asked how her husband was, but he forgot that she was divorced!

► *jihad*—This Arabic word means "a religious war," or a "war for a principle." It can be used in English to mean either "a real war" or "a movement."

The Crusades were a *jihad* of the Middle Ages.

► *junta*—This Spanish word means "a small group of people." It has come to mean a small council of dictators.

The *junta* met for several hours and then decreed an eight o'clock curfew for the capital city.

The school sports club is supposed to be a democracy, but Fidel feels it is run by a *junta* of the football team's best players!

Word History: Like many words in English, this Spanish word comes from the Latin. The Latin word *jungere* means "to join." A *junta* is a group of people who have *joined* together.

► *kibbutz*—This modern Hebrew word refers to an Israeli collective settlement, especially an Israeli collective farm. You may have run across it in newspaper stories about the Middle East.

The residents of the *kibbutz* shared the work of harvesting lemons, cleaning the house, and minding the children.

► *résumé*—This is a good word to know when you are starting to look for work! It is a French word that originally meant "a summing up," and in English has come to mean "a summary of work experience and education that you give to an employer with your job application."

Rosalina's *résumé* describes one summer of waitressing, one summer as a camp counselor, and her volunteer work as a candy striper.

Hint: A *résumé* is a *sum*mary of your work and education.

Warning: Don't confuse *résumé*—with the accent over the *e*—with the English word *resume*. In English, to *resume* something is to begin where you left off.

After lunch, the judge *resumed* the trial.

Sidney finished answering the teacher's question, then *resumed* reading his book.

► *virtuoso*—This Italian word literally means "skilled or learned one." In English, it means "someone who is very skilled technically, especially in the arts"; or it describes a technically skilled performance.

The *virtuoso* picked up his violin and began to play brilliantly, with great bravura.

Jimi Hendrix gave many *virtuoso* performances that were widely admired by other guitarists.

Word History: You can see that the English word *virtuous* is closely related to the word *virtuoso*. Originally, the word meaning "greatly skilled" and the word meaning "of high moral worth" were the same.

Chapter 7:
Words Often Confused
(The Great Meaning Mix-Up)

Some words may be close in meaning, spelling, or sound—but still differ from one another in important ways. Everyone gets these words mixed up once in a while, but if you take the time to glance over these lists, you might realize that you have been confusing some seemingly similar words that are really quite different. Some of these confusing words are presented along with hints for remembering the differences. You might also want to make up your own memory tricks for telling these words apart.

Words That Sound Alike
(Which Witch Ate at Eight?)

Words that sound alike are called *homonyms*. Here are some homonyms—words that sound the same, but have very different spellings and meanings.

▶ *aisle*—a passageway.

▶ *isle*—an island.

There was a wide *aisle* down the middle of the theater, but it was still hard finding a seat in the dark without bumping into someone.

Would you like to sail away to a desert *isle* where you'd never have to do homework again?

Hint: *Isle* is like the word *island*.

► *ascent*—something going up.
► *assent*—to agree to something.

The plane's *ascent* into the clouds was smooth and swift.

Will you *assent* to holding the party at your house if we agree to clean up afterward?

Note: The antonym of *ascent* is *descent*—the trip downwards. The antonym of *assent* is *dissent* — to disagree with something.

The plane's *descent* onto the runway was bumpy and uncertain.

I must *dissent* from the group's decision. I cannot agree to hire the Screamers for the school dance.

► *coarse*—rough; not smooth.
► *course*—part of a meal; or a place for a race; or a path through something; or a plan of study.

Hortense brushed and combed the hair of the tired horse, noticing how *coarse* and rough it felt.

The elegant restaurant offered snails for its first *course*.

The cross-country *course* was wet and muddy after the rain.

On your *course* through life, be sure to plan for emergencies.

Jerome Farr is taking a *course* in first aid to be on the safe side.

► *compliment*—praise or flattery.
► *complement*—something that *completes* or goes
along with something else.

Larry paid me the nicest *compliment!* He said he always enjoys talking with me because I am so interesting.

These chips are a nice *complement* to that guacamole dip—the other chips were too salty.

Mara and Fred *complement* each other's personality—she is very adventurous, and he has a lot of quiet common sense.

Hint: A <u>complement</u> completes something. Also, a comp<u>le</u>ment goes to<u>ge</u>ther with something.

► *hall*—passageway.
► *haul*—to drag or pull something.

Mei Ling stood in the *hall* outside the classroom, wondering how to explain being late.

The mules on the Erie Canal used to *haul* ships through the water.

Words That Sound Similar, But Not the Same (How to Tell Them Apart)

Some words are pronounced somewhat, but not exactly, like other words. It can be easy to confuse both the pronunciation and the meaning of these words. Check the dictionary if you are unsure of the pronunciations of any of the following words: (For more on pronunciation, see Chapter 8.)

► *conscience*—ideas that a person has about
right and wrong.
► *conscious*—being aware or awake.

I wanted to copy Lou's answers on that test, but my *conscience* wouldn't let me. I knew I was doing the wrong thing, and I would have felt guilty for days while my *conscience* was bothering me.

The doctor worked hard until the patient was *conscious* again. The patient had been made *unconscious* when the brick fell on his head.

► *continual*—action that continues, but with interruptions.
► *continuous*—action that continues without interruptions.

I am tired of your *continual* requests for more money! (The person asking for more money keeps doing it, but perhaps waits for a day or so between requests.)

That *continuous* noise is driving me crazy. (The noise has started and has not stopped or been interrupted.)

► *credible*—believable.
► *credulous*—believing in things far too easily; naive.

Do you think it is *credible* that Pokey will win the track meet? Pokey is confident, but I am not so sure.

Jonathan is a very *credulous* person. I believe you could convince him that the moon was made of green cheese if you worked hard enough.

► *eligible*—able to be chosen.
► *illegible*—unreadable.

Are you *eligible* for the basketball team, or isn't your grade point average high enough?

Gwendolyn Graffiti's handwriting is *illegible*—I can't read a word!

Hint: An <u>e</u>ligible person can be <u>e</u>lected.

- ▶ *emigrate*—to leave your native country in order to settle in another.
- ▶ *immigrate*—to come into a foreign country to live.

My ancestors <u>emigrated</u> *from* Ireland and <u>immigrated</u> *to* the United States.

Hint: Here is a chance to use your knowledge of prefixes to help you remember the meaning of a word. People who <u>e</u>migrate use the prefix *e* = "out from," where as people who <u>i</u>mmigrate use a version of the prefix *in-* ("into"). (The *in-* is changed to *im-* to make the word easier to pronounce.)

- ▶ *persecute*—to oppress or harass someone.
- ▶ *prosecute*—to bring a case or person into court.

Mr. Crabtree seems to want to *persecute* me; he is always calling my parents to complain that I am chasing his dog or walking on his lawn.

Many people came to the United States because they were *persecuted* in their own countries; they may not have been allowed to vote or to follow their own beliefs.

Attorney Susan Wynns decided to *prosecute* the case because she wanted to make an example of the drunk driver.

Hint: You pr<u>o</u>secute something in c<u>o</u>urt.

- ▶ *precede*—to go before something else.
- ▶ *proceed*—to move forward.

Will my biology class *precede* my English class or come after it?

Let us *proceed* with this meeting so we can finish up and go out for pizza!

> **Hint:** Again, you can use your knowledge of prefixes to help you here.
> *pre* = before
> *pro* = forward
> Notice the spelling differences between *cede* and *ceed*.

► *respectfully*—done with respect.

► *respectively*—referring back to several things in the order in which they were mentioned.

The man *respectfully* took off his hat.

Gina, Laurie, and Beth wore red, pink, and blue, *respectively*. (That is, Gina wore red, Laurie wore pink, and Beth wore blue.)

> **Hint:** Someone *respectful* is *full of respect*.
> Don't forget to drop the extra *l*!

► *stature*—someone's or something's height or greatness

► *statue*—an object that usually represents a person or animal.

Over the years that he was president, Abraham Lincoln grew in *stature* (that is, became greater).

There is a *statue* of Lincoln in Washington, D.C.

Chapter 8:
Pronunciation
(How Do You Say It?)

How a word is spoken, or *pronounced*, is its *pronunciation*. Often you may recognize a word on paper but not know how it is pronounced (or you may recognize a word by sound but not know how it is spelled! For more on spelling, see Chapter 9).

Most dictionaries tell you how to pronounce words, but they do so through a system of symbols called *phonetic spelling*. A *phonic* is a unit of sound. *Phonetic spelling* is a way of writing words that shows how they sound.

Many languages do not need phonetic spelling because every letter is pronounced the same way all the time. However, English, because it comes from so many different languages, has many different types of pronunciation. If you see the letter *a*, for example, do you pronounce it like the *a* in father, like the *a* in age, or like the *a* in half? If you see the combined letters *ea*, do you pronounce them like dear or like the past-tense word read? How does adding an *e* to the end of a word change its pronunciation? As you already know, the rules will take you only so far. This is because the exceptions to the rules of English pronunciation are almost as numerous as the rules themselves.

For example, look at the nonsense word below:
ghoti

How would you pronounce this?

Well, one old joke says that you might pronounce it *fish—gh* as in lau*gh*, *o* as in w*o*men, and *ti* as in mo*ti*on!

The best thing you can do to help yourself with English pronunciation is just to relax. Everyone pronounces some words wrong some of the time, and pronunciations are changing so quickly that even the dictionary can't keep up with the changes. What was considered poor pronunciation ten years ago may be considered perfectly acceptable today. The important thing is to know what you mean and find a relaxed way to communicate it to others.

However, if you do want to check the pronunciation of a word, you can use your dictionary. Most dictionaries have a pronunciation key in the front that shows you how phonetic spellings are pronounced. Many dictionaries have pronunciation keys on the bottom or top of each page for quick reference. (Most thesauruses do not include pronunciation information.) A pronunciation key might look something like this:

Symbol	Sample Words
a	carrot, fat
ā	say, pray
ä	ah, car, father
e	then, ten
ē	evening, three

Symbol	Sample Words
i	h<u>i</u>s, h<u>i</u>m
ī	l<u>ie</u>, h<u>igh</u>
ō	l<u>ow</u>, s<u>o</u>
o	c<u>o</u>rn, c<u>a</u>ll
ōō	b<u>oo</u>t, S<u>ue</u>
oo	b<u>oo</u>k, p<u>u</u>ll
yōō	v<u>iew</u>, <u>u</u>se
yoo	c<u>ure</u>, s<u>ure</u>
oi	<u>oi</u>l, j<u>oi</u>nt
ou	<u>ou</u>t, l<u>ou</u>d
u	<u>u</u>p, c<u>u</u>t
~~ur~~	f<u>ur</u>, p<u>er</u>son
uh	a in <u>a</u>head
	e in rec<u>e</u>nt
	i in van<u>i</u>ty
	o in c<u>o</u>mpare
	u in foc<u>u</u>s
b	<u>b</u>ack, <u>b</u>arn
d	<u>d</u>og, ba<u>d</u>
f	<u>f</u>ast, o<u>ff</u>
g	<u>g</u>o, ho<u>g</u>
h	<u>h</u>i, <u>h</u>appy
j	<u>j</u>unior, <u>j</u>ar
k	<u>k</u>iss, ta<u>ck</u>
l	<u>l</u>ose, fa<u>ll</u>

106

Symbol	Sample Words
m	<u>m</u>an, wo<u>m</u>an
n	<u>n</u>o, ca<u>n</u>
p	<u>p</u>ack, to<u>p</u>
r	<u>r</u>ed, ca<u>r</u>
s	<u>s</u>et, me<u>ss</u>
t	<u>t</u>ake, ca<u>t</u>
v	<u>v</u>an, ha<u>v</u>e
w	<u>w</u>ear, al<u>w</u>ays
y	<u>y</u>et, on<u>i</u>on, can<u>y</u>on
z	<u>z</u>ebra, ja<u>zz</u>
ch	<u>ch</u>oose, ar<u>ch</u>
sh	<u>sh</u>ake, cra<u>sh</u>
th	<u>th</u>in, tru<u>th</u>
<u>th</u>	<u>th</u>en, fa<u>th</u>er
zh	plea<u>s</u>ure, trea<u>s</u>ure
ng	ri<u>ng</u>, dri<u>n</u>k

► *accuracy*—ak′yuhr uh sē (*not* ak′ruh-sē)
> the quality of being precise or exact.
Scientific research requires great *accuracy*.

► *actual*—ak′cho͞o wuhl *or* ak′sho͞o wuhl
> existing in reality or at the present time.
The *actual* state of affairs is very different from what
you might think.

► *archives*—är′kīvz (*not* ar′chīvz)
> records.
I went down to the city *archives* to look up my birth
certificate.

► *chasm*—kaz'm (*not* chaz'm)
>> a huge gap or crater in the earth; or a big division.

Lin stood in front of the huge *chasm* and tried to shout across to the other side, but the gap was too wide.

► *coup*—koo (*not* koop)
>> a French word that has passed into English; it originally meant "blow." In English it means "a successful action."

If you can really get Peter Plastic and the Compact Disks to play at our high-school dance, it will be a real *coup*.

► *mischievous*—mis'chi vuhs (*not* mis chē' vē uhs)
>> playfully naughty.

The *mischievous* child tied together the laces of all the shoes in the house.

► *omnipotent*—äm nip' uh tuhnt (*not* äm ni pō' tuhnt) all-powerful.

An *omnipotent* ruler can not be challenged by any of his or her subjects.

► *genuine*—jen' yōō wuhn (*not* jen' yōō wīn)
>> real; true.

This coat is made of *genuine* leather, which is why it costs more than the coat made of imitation leather.

► *stipend*—stī' pend *or* stī' puhnd (*not* sti' pend)
>> a regular payment.

The college student received a small *stipend* for living expenses.

Chapter 9:
Spelling
(How Do You Spell It?)

The problem with spelling rules in English is that they take you only so far. For every rule, there are often several exceptions. Sometimes it seems that there are more words that come under the exceptions than come under the rules!

The reason for English's difficult spelling is the huge number of languages that have gone into producing modern-day English. Languages that come only from one source often have more regular spellings than English does. What English loses in spelling difficulties it more than makes up in the richness and variety of words. Still, what do you do about spelling?

The best thing you can do is try to memorize those rules that help, while knowing that you might have to keep "bending" the rules to make room for the exceptions. Here are a few spelling hints that may help:

Adding Prefixes
(Does the Spelling Change?)

Usually adding a prefix to a word does not change the spelling of either the prefix or the word. That means if the prefix ends with a vowel, there will *not* be a double consonant after the prefix: *recommend,* not *reccommend; depress,* not *deppress.*

What if the prefix ends with an *s?* Well, if the word that the prefix is attached to begins with an *s,* then there will be a double *s* (the first *s* ends the prefix, and the second *s* begins the word). If the word that the prefix is attached to does *not* begin with an *s,* then there will not be a double *s.*

No Double *s*	Double *s*
mis apply	mis spell
mis take	dis service
dis ease	dis solve

However, here is something that may be tricky: sometimes the last letter of the prefix is changed in order to make the word easier to pronounce. In that case, you will see a double letter after the prefix:

in + migrate = immigrate
(but e + migrate = emigrate)

in + legible = illegible
(but e + ligible = eligible

con + laborate = collaborate
(but e + laborate = elaborate)

Adding Endings: Words of Two or More Syllables (To Double or Not to Double, That Is the Question)

In the cases of words that have more than one syllable and that end with one vowel plus one consonant, here is a pattern that is usually followed: